A Naked Tree

A Naked Tree

Love Sonnets to C. S. Lewis
and Other Poems

JOY DAVIDMAN

Edited by

DON W. KING

WILLIAM B. EERDMANS PUBLISHING COMPANY
GRAND RAPIDS, MICHIGAN / CAMBRIDGE, U.K.

© 2015 Don W. King
All rights reserved

Published 2015 by
Wm. B. Eerdmans Publishing Co.
2140 Oak Industrial Drive N.E., Grand Rapids, Michigan 49505 /
P.O. Box 163, Cambridge CB3 9PU U.K.

Printed in the United States of America

20 19 18 17 16 15   7 6 5 4 3 2 1

Library of Congress Cataloging-in-Publication Data

Davidman, Joy.
  [Poems. Selections]
  A naked tree: love sonnets to C. S. Lewis and other poems / Joy Davidman;
  edited by Don W. King.
    pages   cm
  Includes index.
  ISBN 978-0-8028-7288-3 (cloth: alk. paper)
  1. Lewis, C. S. (Clive Staples), 1898-1963 — Poetry. 2. Love poetry.
  3. Sonnets.   I. King, Don W., 1951- editor.   II. Title.
  III. Title: Love sonnets to C. S. Lewis.

  PS3507.A6659A6   2015
  811'.52 — dc23

                                                    2015004710

www.eerdmans.com

To David, Jerry, and Warren

Contents

Acknowledgments

I have many people to thank for helping make this book a reality. First, I thank David and Douglas Gresham, who gave me permission to publish their mother's poems. In addition I thank the staff of the Marion E. Wade Center, particularly Laura Schmidt and Marjorie L. Mead, who encouraged my research and provided invaluable assistance during my many visits to the Wade Center. Elizabeth Pearson, the Library Director at Montreat College, and her staff were endlessly patient and helpful in securing materials, especially Nathan King and Martha Martin. I also thank Marshall Flowers, Provost of Montreat College, for granting me release time on several different occasions so that I could complete this book. Also I am most appreciative of the excellent editorial advice of Wm. B. Eerdmans Publishing Company, especially Jon Pott, Vice-President and Editor in Chief, and my editor, Jenny Hoffman. In addition, I thank my editorial assistants Mary Willis Bertram, Laura Davidson, Molly-Kate Garner, Corrie Greene, Alyssa Klaus, and Mackenzie May. Finally, I owe my wife, Jeanine, a great debt since I spent so many hours away from her while working on this book.

All poems by Joy Davidman are copyrighted by David and Douglas Gresham and are used by their permission.

Introduction

Although Joy Davidman (1915-1960) published an impressive quantity of prose — two novels, *Anya* (1940) and *Weeping Bay* (1950); over ninety essays and reviews for the *New Masses*, the semi-official magazine of the Communist Party of the United States of America (CPUSA); and her personal reflections on the Ten Commandments, *Smoke on the Mountain* (1955) — her real gift was poetry.[1] Until recently this was a difficult claim to substantiate. Despite the fact that before she turned twenty-one she had published poems in the prestigious journal, *Poetry*,[2] and less than three years later her only volume of poetry, *Letter to a Comrade* (1938), won the Russell Loines Memorial award for poetry given by the National Institute of Arts and Letters,[3] and even though she published another thirty poems in magazines and book collections, her total of just over seventy published poems was a thin corpus by which to measure her verse. However, in 2010 scores of previously unknown poems were uncovered.[4] Of special interest is

---

1. I offer a comprehensive discussion of Davidman as a writer in *Yet One More Spring: A Critical Study of Joy Davidman* (Grand Rapids: Eerdmans, 2015).

2. "Resurrection" and "Amulet" appeared in *Poetry* 47 (January 1936): 193-95.

3. *Letter to a Comrade* (New Haven: Yale University Press, 1938).

4. Also recovered in these papers were manuscript versions of dozens of short stories, her unpublished novella *Britannia over Brooklyn*, and twenty-seven previously unknown letters from Davidman to her husband, William Lindsay Gresham; her sons, David and Douglas; and her cousin, Renée Pierce — all written between August and December 1952 during her initial trip to England to meet C. S. Lewis. In brief, the story of how these manuscripts came to light is as follows. In the early summer of 2010 Douglas Gresham, Joy Davidman's younger son, was contacted by an ailing Jean Wakeman, who asked him to come and clean out her house after she moved into a

an index by Davidman of the titles of over 230 poems that she dates as having been written between August 1933 and January 1941. The poems are listed in chronological order; in addition, she indicates the number of lines contained in each poem. A second index of sixty-five poems is also among these recovered papers, as well as several dozen additional poems not listed in either of these indices. In all, these poems span the years 1929 to 1955 and provide a rich cache of material by which to offer an updated evaluation of Davidman's poetry.[5]

These recovered poems, along with her published poems, comprise a remarkable body of work. A *Naked Tree: Love Sonnets to C. S. Lewis and Other Poems*, showcases Davidman's poetry and, as the first comprehensive collection of her verse, makes the case that her status as a twentieth-century American poet should be re-apprized.

Readers approaching her verse for the first time will discover three overarching themes. First, her poems often concern God, death, and immortality. For instance, "Againrising" imagines Jesus' thoughts while he suffers on the cross; in fact, although Davidman was ethnically a Jew, many of her early religious poems find her engaged in thinking about or imaginatively conversing with Christ. Another poem, "The Lately Dead," laments a group of slain soldiers, affirming that their deaths will not be forgotten, forgiven, or dismissed; although Davidman was an atheist when she wrote this poem, it and many others explore the ways in which the dead still "live on." In

---

care-giving facility. Wakeman, who was Davidman's closest friend in England, spent a career as a motoring journalist. She often drove Davidman to various spots around Oxford, especially after Joy's bone cancer developed. As a young man Gresham often stayed with Wakeman, particularly after the death of his mother. For instance, after Lewis's death she opened her home to Gresham for three years, between 1963 and 1966. According to Gresham, during the process of cleaning out Wakeman's house he came across not only a large cache of his mother's manuscripts that he had forgotten about, but also several manuscripts by Lewis. Regrettably, Wakeman died on August 16, 2010, at St. Luke's Nursing Home in Headington, England. In late 2010 Gresham deposited his mother's manuscripts in the Marion E. Wade Center at Wheaton College, Wheaton, IL. After several months of processing and cataloguing the material, it was first made available to researchers in April 2011. For more on Wakeman's relationship with Gresham, see "Jean Wakeman (1920-2010)," *SEVEN: An Anglo-American Literary Review* 27 (2010): 5.

5. The materials noted in this paragraph are available in the Joy Davidman Papers, 1936-1964, at the Wade Center.

another example, "Yet One More Spring" insists that some part of a woman will haunt her lover long after she is dead: "I would leave you the trouble of my heart / To trouble you at evening; I would perplex you / With lightning coming and going about my head, / Outrageous signs, and wonders."

Second, a substantial portion of her poetry is given over to politics, especially her rejection of capitalism, her support of the Republicans in the Spanish Civil War (1936-1939), her hatred of fascism, and her early support of communism. For example, in "Prayer against Indifference" she calls curses down upon herself should she fail to be outraged by the many social and political injustices intrinsic to capitalism: "And when I wait to save my skin / Break roof and let my death come in." The poignant poem "Near Catalonia" praises the outnumbered and out-equipped Republican soldiers against impossible odds: "If we had bricks that would make a wall we would use them, / But bricks will break under a cannon-ball ... / We have only the most brittle of all things the man, / And the heart the most iron admirable thing of all / And putting these together we make a wall." Her poem "Strength through Joy" parodies Adolf Hitler's swollen self-importance and ironically mocks his call for his fascist followers to worship him:

> I am precious
> and a treasure to women; honor then my knees
> and the clasp of my thighs. And I will give you,
> you, my dear children, my loving children, you
> wearing my symbol on the fat of your arm
> the beautiful moment, the moment of beautiful pain
> with which you burst into flames; the high, the radiant
> and honorable death.

In "Survey Mankind" she offers one of many arguments justifying communism and rallying others to support the CPUSA: "Now with me / bow and set your mouth against America / which you will make free and the treasure of its men, / which you will give to the workers and to those who turn land over with the plow."

Third, the largest body of her verse is devoted to romantic love, focusing upon not only the physical delights of love-making and a fierce desire to possess the beloved, but also the desolation of either broken romances or unrequited longing. "Postscript," perhaps her most explicitly sexually charged poem, records the aftermath of a furious session of love-making that leaves the female speaker longing for more: "and I would love you beloved who leave me here breathless / lying without knowledge of the muscles of your body / but all I want is the sun, but I want earthquake, / but all I want / all I want." Similarly, "Division" expresses the exhilaration of sexual climax: "And so sweetly / We come together; so the clasp, the spasm / Answer each other, suitably invent / Exhaustion sweeter than content." In "Night-Piece" complete possession is the goal: "I shall make rings around you. Fortress / In a close architecture of wall upon wall, / Rib, jointed rock, and hard surrounding steel / Compel you into the narrow compass of my blood / Where you may beat forever and be perfect." On the other hand, a number of poems deal with the pain of a shattered romance, as in "I Hate You for Your Kind Indifference":

> I hate you for your kind indifference
> That tiptoes past the naked thing who cries
> A shocking lust; and, like a man of sense,
> Stares at my passion with a mild surprise;
>
> That will not waste on my humility
> A charitable anger; you are wise.
> If you should strike me you could not be free
> Forever after of forgiving eyes.
>
> I meant to rouse you till your flesh divined
> Behind my eyes the hot and hostile Woman;
> But you are gentle and I am not human;
> The clarity of your Hellenic mind
> Knows me a pitiable amusing thing,
> A trivial insect with a tattered wing.

Perhaps it is not surprising that one who loves so fiercely also despairs and lashes out in hatred when the relationship is over. This certainly is the case in "Obsession": "I have not forgiven my enemy

/ The splendor of the eyes in his skull / Or that his mouth is good to see / Or that his thought is beautiful." Hatred becomes her sustaining force: "And I have kept me warm in the cold / Hating the valor of his mind." Indeed, without hatred she would find it hard to go on: "This hate is honey to my tongue / And rubies spread before my eye, / Sweet in the ear as any song; / What should I do, if he should die?" And in her poems where she is longing for love to be returned by her beloved, she is not above begging. The most striking example of this occurs in one of her love sonnets to C. S. Lewis:

I wish you were the woman, I the man;
I'd get you over your sweet shudderings
In two such heartbeats as the cuckoo sings
His grace-notes in! I play the games I can
With eye and smile; but not in womanhood

Lies power to lay hands on you and break
Your frosty inhibitions; it would take
Centaurs' force, transfusions of sun's blood.

Call it your virtue if you like; but love
Once consummated, we recover from;
Not so, love starved forever. Thus you have,
With this device of coldness, made me tame;
Your whipped adoring bitch, your tethered slave
Led on the twin leashes of desire and shame.

As these examples suggest, Davidman's love poems are open and honest, terse and direct, passionate and intense, confrontational and vulnerable, tender and poignant.

It is important to note that Davidman cut her poetic teeth while writing in the midst of twentieth-century literary modernism. It is not surprising then that her published poetry is marked by the frequent use of free verse. This is evident in *Letter to a Comrade* in poems such as "Letter to a Comrade," "Twentieth-Century Americanism," "Necrophile," "Survey Mankind," "Lament for Evolution," "For the Revolution," "Sorceress Eclogue," "Yet One More Spring," "The

Empress Changes Lovers," and "Jewess to Aryan." Yet this commitment to free verse belied a deeper grounding in older, established literary forms. For instance, ballades, rondeaux, and villanelles appear throughout her corpus, although until now none have been published.[6] Most striking, however, is her fascination with the sonnet; despite the fact that she published only five sonnets during her lifetime, she wrote over ninety, culminating in her powerful and beautiful sequence of forty-five love sonnets to C. S. Lewis. Her fascination with the sonnet led to an amazing well-spring of literary invention. Readers will find in her sonnets not only a poet who works easily within the constraints of the form, but also an impassioned voice that turns sonnets into something akin to personal journal entries.

Of particular interest to many readers will be the forty-five love sonnets Davidman wrote to Lewis. There are two important general observations to make about this sequence. The first concerns matters related to the composition of the sonnets. Most of the sonnets exist in multiple drafts, although the differing versions show little revision — often a word or punctuation mark is the only variance. The varying drafts often carry titles and a handful are dated. Most were written between 1949 and 1954, revealing that some were written well before Lewis and Davidman met. These matters of composition point out, I believe, that the sonnets were initially conceived of as separate poems. It was only at some point later — perhaps when Davidman was especially frustrated by Lewis holding her at arm's length emotionally and physically — that she decided to put the poems together in the sequence as we now have it. One instance arguing for a later pulling together of the separate sonnets into a sequence is most revealing; the last love sonnet in the sequence, XLIV, is dated by Davidman as having been written in November 1939, a decade before she wrote her first letter to Lewis. One conclusion we can draw from this is that the sonnet sequence to Lewis was a deliberate, conscious decision by a gifted artist who wanted the poems to accomplish two things: to indicate boldly her passion for Lewis and to serve as a piece of pointed rhetoric intent on persuading him to return her affections.

---

6. For more on Davidman's use of verse forms, see the Appendix: Poetic Verse Patterns.

Moreover, as an experienced poet, Davidman knew her individual sonnets could be woven together into a sequence that might accelerate the kind of relationship she wanted to have with Lewis. If this is the case, the sequence gives evidence to Davidman as both a clever advocate and a gifted artist.

The second general observation concerns the relationship between the individual sonnets and the sequence as a whole. Although each sonnet is complete in itself — telling, if you will, its own little story — it is easy to discern a larger story or narrative as we read through the sequence. Accordingly within the sequence many of the sonnets are "conversational"; that is, sometimes Davidman is speaking to herself, sometimes to Lewis directly or indirectly, sometimes to God, sometimes to former lovers, sometimes to no one in particular, and sometimes to several of these at the same time. Throughout the sequence her narrative tone or mood vacillates between despair and hope, anger and resignation, desire and shame, longing and self-denial, scheming and confessing, plotting and humiliation, eros and agape, passion and reason, the flesh and the spirit, a fierce desire to possess and a frustrated acquiesce to give up, and desperation and resolution.[7]

In compiling A *Naked Tree*, I have been directed by the following editorial principles. First, whenever possible I have arranged the poems chronologically as they were written. In some cases, particularly the poems appearing in *Letter to a Comrade*, this means that the published version may have appeared much later than when the poem was initially composed; for the reader's convenience I have provided the date when the poem was written at the end of each poem. This is the most important editorial principle I have followed because I want readers to be able to chart Davidman's development and growth as a poet by being able to see easily when each poem was written. In addition, in several cases I have placed undated poems where I believe they were written chronologically; I note these cases by using a question mark next to the date.

Second, the previously published poems I print here follow the versions that first appeared in print, including those appearing in

7. For more on this, see *Yet One More Spring*.

Letter to a Comrade and those published in journals and magazines. In general, I use the title for each poem as it first was published; or in the cases of poems not titled by Davidman, I title the poem according to the first line of the poem.

Third, I have silently corrected obvious misspellings and made occasional minor punctuation changes. In every case I have tried to provide a clean and precise text for each poem.

January 2015
Montreat College
Montreat, NC

Poems 1929-1938

What Spur of Gold Is This That Pricks the Dawn?

What spur of gold is this that pricks the dawn
To further flaming of its fierce desire
Of glory? On the eager winds of morn
Comes blowing down the soul-devouring fire
That keenly lashes the mad spirit higher
And higher yet; the dry hot fever of fame,
The far bright crown to which all slaves aspire —
Need most imperative, to which the name
Of fondest love shows but a flickering flame.

(January 1929)

Sunset — The Hall of Fame

The river is a quiet flicker of gold;
The dropping sun, over the serrate ridge
Of those tall buildings rising thousand-fold
Slants by the far pier of a shadowy bridge.

The trolley rattles home its weary crowd;
The parting rays of sunlight softly gild
The sculptured statesman, watching, almost proud,
The splendid city that he helped to build.

I

Wide eyes carved in bronze quiet, do you see
Towers sky-climbing from the river-side,
This legacy from your firm-molding hand,
This City! — though the murmuring shadow-sea
Has swept you out on its eternal tide,
Changeless deep eyes, you watch our changing land.

(Summer 1929)

In a Moment of Ecstasy

When I am old beside a sheltered fire,
When dim blue shadow fills my passive years,
I would not look upon the sun-desire
Of my keen sunlit youth with helpless tears.

Let me forget the passion of my blood,
If this red passion ends despondent gray!
Do rivers' muddy trickles remember flood,
Proud in hill-cleaving strength, a gayer day?

To feel the slow slide from precarious stars
Down to the placid, safe, ignoble ground
Were harder than, with no brain-searing scars
Of scarlet memory, to call age crowned

With wisdom through mere drowsing of the soul,
Forgetting life's young magic, that life stole.

(Winter 1929-1930)

Endymion: I Had Prayed to the Distant Goddess[1]

I had prayed to the distant goddess all that while,
With the mad wish that Deity would bend,
Stoop to the level of a human love.
And that clear distant silver would not heed
Desire, imperious in its rule of me,
But rode the night down with her pack of stars.

And I knew that I dared the undefied,
That this most magic of the mysteries
Was not as fireflies to catch and crush,
Nor even as the mocking light that lures
A vain pursuit, but was beyond pursuit,
A far-seen vision, throned upon a cloud.

Then the moon answered and came down to me.
Oh — I had lain for many nights and sighed
Because she was no nearer, though I knew
The moon was brighter for the distance. Now
She has come down, the years' dream has come true.
A silver shadow floating above my head,
The cold white moon dissolving in the air,
And dripping liquid silver through the pines,
Till it surrounded me in silver dew,
All of the brightness soft within my arms.

Yet she was magic, high above the pines,
Being divine and unattainable,
And white-serene, while I looked up at her.

(Winter 1929-1930)

---

1. In Greek mythology, the young shepherd prince, Endymion, was loved by Selene, goddess of the moon. When Zeus offered him anything he wanted, he chose an ever-lasting sleep so that he would remain youthful forever. However, Selene visited him every night while he lay asleep in a cave on Mount Latmus in Caria.

3

Midsummer Madness

When the sun poured hot silver on silver-cool water,
    And in green tree-shadow our rowboat lay,
And a brown fly buzzed till you reached and caught her
    What was the dream that caught us, that day?

We were lazy as leaves in the windless willow,
    Summer-drowsy with sunlight and murmuring bees,
Yet I lifted my head from a pine-needle pillow
    To watch a red bird among the trees.

And your eyes were lit with the glancing fire
    Of the blue lake gleaming in hot blue sky,
So, it perched unseen on the warm sweet briar,
    Or fluttered, perhaps, through the reeds near by.

It was nothing brighter than the bright weather,
    No magic more deep than the lake, we knew;
A passion light as a floating feather,
    Born of a hill-lake's noonday blue.

The moon's coin-silver leaves water tainted
    With the moon-mad desire of too many men;
Will the dark lake here ever flash, sun-painted,
    The fire of that brief laughing passion again?

(Summer 1930)

Rondeau of the Rain[2]

The rain is dark against the sky
And sudden silver in the street;
In the pale night two shadows meet.
The rain falls with a silver sigh

And two ghosts walk beneath the high
Chill clouds that shower freezing sleet.
The rain is dark against the sky
And sudden silver in the street.

Under winter rain-clouds fly
Ghosts, on shadow-winged feet,
— Through the live rain, cold and sweet, —
Of two who did not want to die.

The rain is dark against the sky.

(Winter 1930-1931)

Clair de Lune[3]

Your soul is an old garden, where the mad
Masked fauns and idly-graceful dancers go,
Playing a graceful lute, and somehow sad
In their fantastic robes, and singing slow.

All, singing in a minor key a lay
Of conquering love and life and the warm night,
Seem not to believe that they are free and gay,
And their song blends itself with the calm moonlight,

2. Originating as a lyric form in thirteenth-century France, the rondeau was popular among medieval court poets and musicians. The rondeau (French for round) is characterized by the repeating lines of the refrain and by the two rhyme sounds throughout.

3. First published in *Hunter College Echo* (Christmas 1932). The poem is Davidman's translation of Paul Verlaine's poem of the same name.

5

Sad light of the calm moon, crystal and cool,
Which make the quiet birds in the trees dream,
And the tall fountain in the marble pool
Sob with its ecstasy, in the silver gleam.

(Winter 1930-1931)

Odelette[4]

I with just one little reed
Can make the high trees quiver,
And the dew-cool meadow,
And the gentle willow
And the ever-singing river.
I with just this hollow reed
Have awakened the wood to song.
He who passes, he may hear
In the evening, in the wind,
In the silence and his mind,
Far or near,
Faint or strong …
He who passes, dreaming long,
Listening within his mind
He will ever after find
He is listening to my song.

See, I need
Just this hollowed water-weed
(From the fountain where, they say,
Love, one day,
Saw his sad face in the cool
Fragrance of the quiet pool,
In the water, quiet and deep)

4. First published in *Hunter College Echo* (Christmas 1932). The poem is Davidman's
translation of Henri de Regnier's poem of the same name.

To make whoever passes weep,
The grasses shiver,
The sunlit water quiver;
I with just this hollow thing
Have made the ancient forest sing.

(*Winter* 1930-1931)

Symphony in D Minor

Pale stars hide behind the sky.
    Over the trees dark winds are winging.
Over the trees the torn clouds fly;

The long clouds pass like a dim ship bringing
    An insolent princess who scorns the night,
And ghosts of midnight winds are singing.

When the moon arrives the sky is bright
    With clouds of a sad and silver design,
And patterned trees in the moon's pale light

    Drip with the past rain's moonlit wine.

(*Autumn* 1931)

Noyade[5]

I
We were beset by water at our death;
We were stripped upon the naked beach and bound

5. "Noyade" denotes a mass execution of persons by drowning, as practiced at Nantes, France, during the Reign of Terror (1794) and the French Revolution. David-man adds this explanation to this and the following poem: "The French Revolution sometimes bound men and women together and drowned them in the harbor."

And flung to agony; our silver breath
Bubbled and burst in sunlight as we drowned.

The fierce and tortured passion of your dying
Struck at my throat and struggled in my hair,
Until we sank beneath the pointed crying
Of hungry bullets in the hollow air.

The cold dawn glittered on us where we lay —
Pale flame on the tangled corpses in the sand,
Over whom blew the vague and salty spray
To feed the windy forests far inland,

Till bitter blood of these unquiet seas
Ran in the veins of dark and writhing trees.

II
So the vague cruel paradise of dreams
Brought your desired flesh to my embrace
Where silken water wove in subtle lace
Our hair, the seaweed and the lost sunbeams

Wandering in a wilderness of streams;
Brought me death linked in iron to a lover,
A shining bullet and a bitter river
Where drowning bodies swirled in silver gleams.

Sir, though your violent and naked ghost
Came to me cruelly in the tangled night,
You never were my lover; at the most
Your hands were cool and pleasant and polite.
In every way but this the darkness lied;
I dreamed you hurt me even while you died.

(August 1933)

I Hate You for Your Kind Indifference

I hate you for your kind indifference
That tiptoes past the naked thing who cries
A shocking lust; and, like a man of sense,
Stares at my passion with a mild surprise;

That will not waste on my humility
A charitable anger; you are wise.
If you should strike me you could not be free
Forever after of forgiving eyes.

I meant to rouse you till your flesh divined
Behind my eyes the hot and hostile woman;
But you are gentle and I am not human;
The clarity of your Hellenic mind
Knows me a pitiable amusing thing,
A trivial insect with a tattered wing.

(August 1933)

The Difficult Ritual of Your Adoration

The difficult ritual of your adoration
Needs patient lips and serviceable knee,
And the small fluting of my poetry
Tuned for your ear to dulcet admiration.

Whatever light and lovely thing is mine
I burn in pleasant incense for your praise;
My body and my brain, my nights and days,
In sacrificial torture at your shrine.

These fragile aches are an offering
Trivial for my thirsty prayer to bring,
Yet leave your laughter only for a while;

Leave laughter and your hard serenity
Within the polished sky, and pity me
In any way that is without a smile.

(*August 1933*)

The Green and Silken Summer Passes Me

The green and silken summer passes me;
Your silver eyes and your cold yellow hair,
Your eyes, your subtle voice, and if you wear
Straight lips or smiling, leave my memory.

Your eyes I have forgotten, and your hair,
Your lesser ways of laughter. You must be
A blowing ghost across a space of sea
And echoes of a song; your eyes, your hair.

It is the pleasant image of your mind
That I have lost; a lithe malignant pain
Rattles my dry and brittle heart; above
The glassy sky is hollow, bright and blind;
My flesh is still unanswered, and my brain
Still dark and dark. I have not lost my love.

(*August 1933*)

I Know My Eyes Are Like a Dog's

I know my eyes are like a dog's, and plead
Too humbly; still, you fling the dog a bone.
You will not toss me for my eager need
Even the bitter answer of a stone.

I am your starving and devoted slave,
Thus hate you sometimes. At love's other end

I'll set my wits to measuring a grave
For a proud corpse that would not be my friend.

I shall devise your sepulcher, and wear
With hard delight my mourning-colored hair,
As, when the passion of the day is done,
A troubled twilight of fantastic clouds
Shaped like rebellious angels, slowly shrouds
The pearly sun, the somber golden sun.

(August 1933)

If I Contrived Myself a Diamond Death

If I contrived myself a diamond death
Lovely and lit with changing frosty stars,
Or if I wore the stripes and grinning scars
Of savage dying, or gave up my breath

In glamorous agony, my soul might take
Solace that love had gleaming ways to kill;
It would be pretty artistry to spill
My splendid blood in jewels for your sake.

I am destroyed unbeautifully here
By hard and little things rubbed cold and clean;
At spotless tiny tasks I sit between
Cold tea and toast, and with a casual ear
Beneath a clock-face in a shiny room
I hear the crystal ladies tinkling doom.

(August 1933)

Unwary Thirst within My Withering Brain

Unwary thirst within my withering brain
Sips burning honey from the serpent-flowers
Of tangled thought; in slow and icy hours
While I can hear the poisonous blue rain

In idiot whispers at the window-pane,
I half believe I am your enemy;
I plan a variegated agony
To recompense you for my writhing pain.

Your body is as precious as the sun,
A sacred and a salt communion
Denied my loving self, whom to console
I play with hate of you, devising horror,
Nor fear to face within the naked mirror
This aspect of my particolored soul.

(August 1933)

To Decorate My Sorrows

To decorate my sorrows for the keen
Approval of your white aesthetic brain
I weave delectably upon a screen
Minute and silver traceries of pain;

I find a jeweled word for every wound,
Mellow and delicate words which I array
In silken arabesques of tiny sound;
Artist's diversion for a rainy day.

Yet while despair anatomizing passion
Shapes hard and shining poetry, and while
I use my sobbing thought of you to fashion

A sonnet from your casual slight smile,
— An art I try to value high above you —
Even while I write about you, sir, I love you.

(August 1933)

Whom They Destroy

I have grown mad with laughter till I see
A toothy grin of lightning in the dark,
The curious smiling of a hungry shark,
The vast voracious ridicule of the sea,

Where I go down beneath cacophony
Of all my deities in merriment,
Who from the tarnished thunder-clouds are bent
Over their creature. Do not laugh at me.

(October 1933)

Our Shadows Blew Away

Our shadows blew away in air,
Pale, polished, and austere;
We walked incarnate where
All spirits go in fear.

The curious pathways of the sun
Opened softly to our flesh;
Our magic bodies spun
Space in a burning mesh

To capture us within our limbs,
Imprisoned in desire;
We met like severed flames
In a unity of fire.

13

But underneath the sunlight when,
In disenchanted air,
We wake and walk again,
Our shadows will be there.

(*Late Autumn* 1933)

Endymion: The Upright Forest Closes[6]

The upright forest closes
My journey in with bars;
The formal night opposes
Geometry of stars

To my intense unreason;
And the wind weaves
An unrelenting prison
With the black shapes of leaves.

Like ghosts in wizard cages,
Entangled in a rune,
My captive spirit rages
And cannot find the moon.

(*December* 1933)

---

6. This poem was originally included in the manuscript of *Letter to a Comrade* (hereafter *Letter*) but was removed at the suggestion of Davidman's editor, Stephen Vincent Benét; see her letter to Benét of July 25, 1938, in *Out of My Bone: The Letters of Joy Davidman*, 12 (hereafter *Bone*). The poem was first published in *Bone*, 9-10. For more on Endymion, see note 1 above concerning "Endymion: I Had Prayed to the Distant Goddess."

Resurrection[7]

Pain cannot contrive for you
Humility beyond your own,
Stripped of your body to the bone.
Passion will not weave anew
A fabric more than skeletal
To veil the candor of your skull.

Fire and anger let you rest;
The wind comes where your lips are mute,
Blowing a labyrinthine flute
Out of the caverns of your breast.
Fire and agony depart
From fallen ashes of a heart.

This is the kingdom that you find
When the brave empty eye-holes stare
Impartially against the air;
A little universe defined
By infinite white ribs for bars
Against the struggles of the stars.

This is the power that you hold
Over these worlds of splintered sand:
Your crystal framework of a hand
Can crumple space in hollow cold,
And your small broken fingers roll
The seven heavens in a scroll.

This is the glory that you have:
A broad sun standing overhead

---

7. First published in *Poetry* 47 (January 1936): 193-94. A longer version of the poem
was originally included in the manuscript of *Letter* (see *Bone*, 6-8) but was removed at
the suggestion of Stephen Vincent Benét; see Davidman's letter to Benét of July 25,
1938, in *Bone*, 12.

To shape a halo for your head;
Skies wheel and laugh above a grave
To worship, in the fields of breath,
Inviolable lovely Death.

Symbols for the celebrant
Are your sharp and silver feet,
Syllables he shall repeat;
So your light bones lie aslant
The mystical and sacred sun —
Infinity in skeleton.

(Easter 1934)

Sonnet for Ariel[8]

Nympholept of loveliness
When the petals of the moon
Brighten to the wind's caress
In the mellow afternoon,
And the light lies motionless
Toward the sunset in a swoon,
Let the great faint odorless
Lilies wake you with a tune!

Hear a silver flower-bell
Summon spirits to arise!
Summer stars and fireflies
Laugh to lead you, Ariel,
Where the proud and leopard skies
Prowl with thunder in their eyes.

(Easter 1934)

8. Here Davidman alludes to Ariel, one of the main characters in William Shakespeare's *The Tempest.* In the play Ariel is a spirit who has been freed from imprisonment in a tree by Prospero; out of thanks and some coercion, Ariel serves Prospero and carries out his commands.

Ducdame[9]

Green leaves make patterns in my mind,
And ever after
Swift arabesques of shining trees are stenciled
Over the blind
Wild whorls of sunlight that the sky has penciled
Upon your darkness shaken by a laughter.
Will you wear
A laugh forever shining in your hair?
For I can see
Only the image that my soul believes,
A doubtful mouth and an inveterate tree,
A sad man in a pattern of green leaves.   (Easter 1934)

And Rainbow Wings

If in my dream you wore a monstrous shape,
Some unimaginable beast of death
To part my little body and my breath,
An iron dragon or distorted ape;

If your strong semblance came in lust to rape
A flesh that flowers to this consummation,
Or brought an illusory adoration,
Sleep would become enchantment and escape.

The pageantry of the fantastic night
Advances in a wan investiture,
The sunless color that my eyes endure
When cold awake I seek you in the night;
And when my dreaming speaks I hear the gray
And casual echo of your voice by day.   (May 1934)

9. In Act II, scene 5 of Shakespeare's As You Like It, Jaques defines ducdame as "a Greek invocation to call fools into a circle."

Meteorite

Now the splendid wound you wear
Brightens you a little while;
Agony will gild your hair,
Elaborate your smile.

Miracles and fires hive
In the tunnels of your brain;
You are stranger than alive,
Deified by pain.

Iron planets in the skies
Flare like glory and are spent;
You will not eternalize
The sun impermanent.

Eddies of electric hate,
Lights and colors of desire
Leave your body desolate;
Never hinder fire.

Constellations die into
Tangled slag and broken stone;
So you find the shell of you
Brittle as a bone.

So you find your halo fled,
Aureoling other stars,
Leaving you a flesh too dead
For splendor and for scars.

Tarnished metal green and black
Flowered in the sky before
Creation broke upon a rack
To quench a meteor.

So a slack reality
Lying empty and content
Saves your soul from ecstasy;
If a lightning sent

Out of trouble and the den
Of volcanoes in the moon
Strikes you into fire again
May it not be soon.

(September 1934)

I Am Not Answerable

I am not answerable for delight
To your attrition of my skin and soul
That makes the hot and heavy animal
An inconsiderable rag of white.

I have stripped open to you day and night;
Against this colorless and casual
Devouring of myself essential
My leavings are not curious to fight.

Take all the entity; it is not much;
When my desires and I are drained away,
A tinted sky on any empty day,
An alchemy of pretty taste or touch
Can wake such answers in it as contrive
To prove my body still a flesh alive.

(September 1934)

Odi et Amo[10]

I would have given you this flower or that,
Tears for your pleasure, roses for your grief,
Would bind my precious hair into a mat

Before your feet, or bring a silken leaf
To kiss your thirsty mouth away from dearth;
Would bind my thoughts into a summer sheaf

Of corn arisen from a barren earth
To nourish you forever; and would bend
This fire to sing contentment on your hearth.

This little pleading image of your friend,
This fabric knit and riveted for life,
I would have brought you, careless of the end;

A flare of laughter, and a fancy rife
With spirits to inform the silver breath;
All this for love; for this ungentle strife

I shall find present ways to give you death.

(October 1934)

---

10. The title means "I hate and I love." First published in *Poetry* 49 (March 1937): 327.

Witch in the City[11]

Incessant rooftops to the sky
Spatter their insensate cry
Where the planets circling sing;
There on evanescent wing
Miracles of silver and steel
Unimaginably reel
Over cloud and under sun
Till the yellow day is gone.
Then the moon alight and thin,
Fish with an enchanted fin,
Swims into a starry mesh,
Luring soul and loosing flesh
Till the body is of air
Garlanded with comet's hair;
Till the spirit may endure
Images that flower obscure
Over facets of the brain;
Strange concrete of joy and pain,
Hooded horrors out of night;
Then the streets are waste and white,
Pallid doorways to a tomb,
Then apparelled in the gloom
My enfranchised ghost shall fly
Painting death across the sky.

(November 1934)

---

11. This poem was originally included in the manuscript of Letter (see Bone, 9) but was removed at the suggestion of Stephen Vincent Benét; see Davidson's letter to Benét of July 25, 1938, in Bone, 12.

Amulet[12]

I am a serpent that will suck your blood,
Sting your bare eyes, or pleasurably drain
Sweet fiery thought and honey from your brain,
And find the savor of your heartstrings good.

I will unclothe your spirit of your skin,
If I can take your body in the snare
That out of flowers and my flowering hair
And idle night these incantations spin.

This is the way to keep your soul from me;
Let the sweet lure and the entangled guile
Crumble before your tolerant clear smile;
And let your cold and lovely honesty
Within my semblance made of shallow glass
Read my desires of you as they pass.

(December 1934)

Thunderbird

Where darker trees oppose
The brilliant sand,
A bird will open and close
Like a spasmodic hand.

The color of the sun
Alters the sky
To the sharp arch of stone
Split open with a cry.

A wheeling voice has found
Dominion where

12. First published in *Poetry* 47 (January 1936): 194-95.

Incendiary sound
Lights up the air.

(January 1935)

Dedication

If you so far forget your constant mind,
If you look up and listen to the wind
Because your careful ear detects a cry;
It is a bird's voice wandering in the sky,
It is a wandering bird, it is not I!

(August 1935)

The Half-Hearted[13]

I would not give my body to the fangs
Of lightning, nor to windy snow, nor hiss
Of serpent-lovely flame, to spare him pangs;
And yet I love my love no less for this.

Air, and the waters, oceans of old fire
Crusted like rubies in the core of earth,
Sprout their thin tendrils into my desire;
My passion goes to hatch a world to birth,

Such flickerings light up the opal mind;
Such blood and color am I master of;
I have created mountains and designed
Cold flowerings of frost to please my love.

I give the sorceries that I have written,
My sharp and subtle arabesques of wit;

13. First published in Poetry 49 (March 1937): 325.

Is there an alchemy I have forgotten?
Is there a sacrament that I omit?

Will he not take the spices and the honey
And the sharp frankincense upon his altar?
Spare the poor life and love the silver money?
Accept the flesh, although the spirit falter?

The harsh imperial carving of his head
Will never turn its marble to a kiss
Though my soft mouth were singing or were dead;
And yet I love my love no less for this.

(*November 1935*)

Miss Briggs' Farm

A passionate twilight flares and darkens slowly;
Her sweet earth breathes, her filmy waters ripple;
This is her bread and salt and fruitage wholly.

The heavy flesh of farmland like a nipple
Breaks into pointed rooftops and sharp towers
Discreetly phallic, and the birdwings stipple

Their shifting figures through the various hours
Upon a sky as shrill as bluejays flying;
Arrogant birds unclose like ardent flowers

On clouds, so cut to patterns with their crying,
That dwindle into hollow air, and after
The peacock light comes to his lovely dying

In western rays of long and slanting laughter,
And doubtful musical delights awaken,
She stares for comfort at the present rafter

And crossbeam of the roof that she has taken
To stand between her and an echoing starlight;
In the cool copulating world, forsaken

Of the male thigh and sinew, stinging hair bright
And tender, strong male pitiable hands,
Her spirit in the insubstantial firelight

Glimpses a vague loss, fumbles with the bands
Woven to throttle her against desire;
But this is all, or all she understands.

She has no faces for her busy fire
To tease her memory with; it is contriving
A patient serpent that will sway no higher

Under her hand, for all his writhen strivings;
She is well served tonight by flame and passion
Turned into household beasts and fit for driving.

For she will feed in an ecstatic fashion
Her secret body, delicate and fierce;
Grown tired of the barren scourge and lashing

And dry austerities of ordered years,
She goes, naked and shuddering and white,
As silverly as subtle lightnings pierce

Blackness, and filigree the shuttered night,
And silently laugh; and she without a sound
Passes; spread out in cruciform delight,

Upon a hill her body clasps the ground,
Devising for her an ambiguous sinning,
With the keen arrow of her breast to wound

The satiating earth; she feels it spinning,

While the sharp lights of stars hold to their places
Steadily, till a silent dawn beginning

Turns the dim nightly rocks to staring faces
That hate a woman for her subtle pleasure;
She slips from tangles of the world's embraces,

Compels her limbs into a narrow measure,
And so steps warily in morning dew,
Cooing to memory cradled like a treasure.

(December 1935)

The Gypsy's Song

I love men for little things;
Not the jewels in their rings,
Not their ape and peacock power
Shall enchant me for an hour;
Nor shall wisdom ever take me;
Those have wisdom who forsake me.
Nor may trumpets of romance
Ever lead my love a dance;
Though he wear a pretty hide
I'll not purr against his side.

I love men for little things;
Hands as delicate as wings,
Hands as strong as yellow fire
Strike a spark to my desire;
Curve of eyebrow, cut of cheek
Make my supple knees grow weak;
Dagger slapping on his thighs,
Murderous splendor in his eyes,
Twisted laughter at his mouth
Prove my blood is of the south.

I love men for lesser things
Than the painted dust on wings
Fastened to a butterfly;
Long small skeletons am I
Amorous of, with built on these
Bodies leaner than the trees;
Long throats modeled cleverly could
Send hot bubbles through my blood,
Crisp voices and rough murmurings;
These are the gypsy's lovely things.

(December 1935)

Second Gypsy's Song

I am not more precious than rubies,
I cannot cook you a dinner,
And only adorable boobies
Could think me less than a sinner;
I am not as gold as the morning
Nor as proud as God or the Devil;
Nor am I fit for adorning
A nunnery or a revel.

I cannot give you sorrow,
I only give you laughter;
From sunset till tomorrow
Our love grows daft and dafter;
With your virtuous notions a-tipsy,
To have me for your lover,
You'll merrily follow the gypsy
The wanton world over.

(January 1936)

Variations on a Theme[14]

Non omnis moriar;[15]
But in the crystal chill
Where wrinkled worlds are still,
Smiling at naked sky
My soul shall lie,
Discarnate, discreate,
Too tenuous for fate,
And too bereft of blood
For the abhorrent God
To tatter and mar.
Non omnis moriar.

But floating and alone
This silver essence, grown
Silver as rain,
Shall be loosed of pain;
No dark shall blind
The spirit so fined,
Elate and fluid stuff;
It will pierce the rough
And pitiable shell
Left empty as a bell;
I shall wear a star;
Non omnis moriar.

My wings shall be alight,
Transcending night;
And figures of thin fire
Shall hover in a choir
To garland me around
With sweet frail sound.
More delicate than breath

14. First published in Poetry 49 (March 1937): 323-24.
15. Latin for "I shall not wholly die."

I shall flit out of death;
The tinsel soul shall go
Higher than mountain snow
Into the windy air;
Non omnis moriar.

If when a grave awakes
This egg of dreaming breaks,
And our brittle selves when they die
Abjure the sky,
And spirits feed, earthbound,
The despicable ground,
Yet lovelier grasses grow
From subtler earth below;
From this earth I cry.
I shall not wholly die
While death begets a flower;
Non omnis moriar.

(February 1936)

Shadow Dance[16]

The hurtful power of flesh
Lends your desire a mesh
And your hatred a blade;
You lunge, where unafraid
I flash and evade.

So you will swirl your net,
Intent to set
Strong toils about my head
And strike me dead,
Who presently am fled

16. First published in *Poetry* 49 (March 1937): 326.

Shifty as little sand
Blown from a closed hand;
Too lunar and thin
To fix upon a pin,
My trophy skin

Will not adorn a wall.
You cast your net, and fall;
Now admirably strain
At the slim noose of pain;
You will not fight again.

(May 1936)

Regrets

Winter and summer
Like wind blow over;
Let the first comer
Make you his lover.

Snow in April
Is gone as soon
As seeds of maple
Or honey in June.

Rain will ruin you,
Laughter will fade;
Life goes askew in you
If you're a maid.

Summer and winter
Pass in the sky;
Let your heart splinter
For the first passer-by.

(May 1936)

Villanelle of Moonlit Sea[17]

Like patterns of moons across the sea
The flying fishes glimmer and skip
Drunk on the moon and ecstasy.

The frothy eyes of ripples see
Fishwing and birdwing glide or dip
Like patterns of moons across the sea.

Wave and wind illusively
Make flurries of a silver whip,
Drunk on the moon and ecstasy,

And the small waters flickering flee
Silkily parted from a ship,
Like patterns of moons, across the sea.

Sharply the tide curves silently
Moonward over the pale world's lip,
Drunk on the moon and ecstasy.

Icily bursts an entity
Into a million shapes that slip
Like patterns of moons across the sea,
Drunk on the moon and ecstasy.

(May 1936)

---

17. A villanelle is a nineteen-line poem with two repeating rhymes and two refrains. The poem is composed of five tercets and a final quatrain. The first and third lines of the opening tercet are repeated alternately in the last lines of the succeeding stanzas. In the final quatrain, the refrain serves as the poem's two concluding lines.

Heortes Helen[18]

Never forgotten,
Frail air blown by
Drifts thin satin
Clouds on the sky.

Never remembering
Festering pain,
Echoes, trembling
Silverly, rain.

Wind will cover you;
Rain will hide;
Healing will glide

Silkily over you;
Under sun
Pain will be gone.

(*June* 1936)

Optic Nerve

A portent is a lovely thing;
A liquid look in the sun; a swirl
Of leaping threads of air; a ring
Of vague and variable pearl
Decking the stars, transforming sight
To something lunatic and bright.

The pale air swells; dilating skies
Of a perverse and friendly shape
Grow swimmingly before your eyes;

18. The title means "hidden, secret, or concealed heart."

Into the clouds a soft escape
Is offered you who snarl and reel
At the shrill accuracies of steel.

How idly and gracefully
The coarser glares of faces die
Into a light monotony
Of moons; and delicate and shy
The shadows edge into your mind;
Then you discover you are blind.

(October 1936)

Chimaera

My heart is hollow,
My bones are thin;
Your hand can follow
My ribs out and in.

No matter how fiercely
And sweetly you stare
My flesh will scarcely
Obstruct the air;

Fanged like the frost
In winter, eyed
Like your own ghost
Perished of pride,

I make a limber
Silhouette
You will not remember
And cannot forget.

(October 1936)

Hymn of Private Hate

More than my enemies' worst sins
I loathe the sound of violins;
Whose tricky spangling of the air
With tinsel scatterings of star
And trivialities of pain
Apes the smooth melancholy of rain;
The easy insinuating sound
That tinkles, saddening the ground,
Contriving prettily a brief
Similitude of pleasant grief.

Remote and bloodless miracles,
Each note as separate as bells,
The icy fiddles clean and bright
Include the stars, omit the night.
A soul more soft and reasonable
Than angels sweetly mocking hell,
A small and false humanity,
Lives in the hollow slice of tree
And snapping wire; where no uncouth
Agony ever finds a mouth
To bellow; where no sorrows thrive
And only sweetness is alive.
Yet none the less a languorous tone
Of something whining and alone,
Sick, glutinous, obscene, will gloat
Out of the strings as from a throat
Mellowed to thick and tragical
Exalted sobs of alcohol.

Was ever any passion thin
Enough to feed the violin
That dares to stale it, make of it
An ecstasy so counterfeit,
So delicate, so soothing, pleasing,

Detestable and tender, teasing
Small amorous contortions from
Music meant as curt as a drum?
No human singing which proceeds
Of perilous flesh that sweats or bleeds
Attains this satin eloquence;
No fierce orchestral weapons, tense
And dark artillery of sounds,
Prick us with these sugared wounds.
Skating arpeggios[19] on a skin
Glassy and fine, the violin
Will not break his ice to free
The angry and harmonious sea.   (December 1936)

Elizabethan

I will love you no more;
I have loved you so long
That I, born strong,
A reveler in war
And a fighter in wine,
Now dwindle and pine
Like a dream in the sun;
Let loving be done.

I will hate you no more;
I have hated so long
That my mind is gone wrong,
Corrupted, and sore;
My soul is drawn thin
As a silver wire pin
And vicious as a gun;
Let hating be done.

19. In an arpeggio, the notes of a chord are played in rapid succession instead of
simultaneously.

I am I!
I have no need of you
Any more than the sky
Or what god may peer through
His blue lens at the skull
Of the earth; I am all
That is, that I need;
I never will bleed
Precious dribbles of pain
For a lover again;
Let me sleep, let me eat,
My sole body tastes sweet,
If I live I am free;
You get no more of me.   (March 1937)

Walpurgisnacht[20]

Let the dear wind go over your head
nor answer whatever cries on the wind
naming your name, nor find
wraith of a living man or ghost of a dead
lamenting in a voice more profound than wind
and made like a simulacrum[21] of the air
on any night in your bed;
for this is no more than disembodied air
that breathes upon your eyes and again so lightly
makes whispers delicately in your hair,
whatever susurrus[22] wordless in your ear
wears voices nightly;
nor ever any carnal body slightly
foreshadowed climbs the hollow air,
nor any spirit riding in the air.   (April 1937)

20. Walpurgisnacht is the eve of May Day, when witches were thought to ride to prearranged meetings.
21. A material image, made as a representation of some deity, person, or thing.
22. A soft murmuring or rustling sound.

Weltschmerz[23]

Farewell the lonely soul,
Complete within its own
Caparison of bone,
A virtuous miracle

Of all good joy and peace;
That never need sustain
The violence of pain
Wrung from an alien face,

Sucking a separate life;
Farewell that spirit alone
In diverse wars, his own
Armor, and his own knife.

Now welcome tangled eyes,
Welcome tumultuous air;
Where many millions are
None solitary dies;

Confusion shall contrive
In this monastic brain
The busy numerous pain
Of everything alive.

(April 1937)

Suggestions

The clouds break softly
Over the sun;
Silver and shiftily
Flashes run

23. A mood of sentimental sadness.

Leaving like tender
Waves a little stirred
A line more slender
Than any bird

And broadening wearily
As less than light
Where the moon eerily
Hints at night.

(April 1937)

Carillons[24]

Frail as glass bells the bright sky
tinkles; lightly falling the glitter
trills a little; sun shaken on a stem of air
clamors in gold.
The leaves of many trees being green as hammered gold
sawtoothed and thin, speak metal whispers
and light runs over them; from the metal leaves
rebounding, shrill fragmentary silvered sunlight
cries a million times in the air.

Out of a brazen throat the sun arising
shouts, and a thick chant of dust
thunders at the sky, and all the world's a clangor
when presently the stormclouds distend and resound,
the iron air like cannon sends loud destruction
crashing at the walls of earth.
Yet after these angers, after the voice of lightning,
after the proud bells of thunder and the bells of the rain,

24. A carillon is a set of fixed bells chromatically tuned so as to produce concordant harmony when many bells are played together. The bells are sounded by hammers controlled from a keyboard.

the jangling darkness, hesitating the moon
sings like a bird.

(*May* 1937)

Down among the Nazis

When the world weighs too much
The soul's escape
Must be to love and clutch
A fouler shape;

Denied by human eyes
The flesh is eased
When the vile body lies
Down with the beast;

And we who live aloof
From any starry thing
Love Satan for his hoof
And hate him for his wing.

(*November* 1937)

Marriage Service

Perceive the lovely fact of bone
And blood and fingernails and hair
Contrived of rain and nursed on stone,
Pleasant earth, and a little air.

Possess for once the actual
Thinking bubble in your two hands
And love the pretty miracle
As any skull alive demands,

And take the forking of its thighs
Between your thighs and never say
A stranger kennels in its eyes
In any hour of night or day.

(December 1937)

Poetess

She is too tired for poetry; give over,
Sad throat, bewildered brain,
Leave the war for the dead and night for the lover,
Spare the pain.

Too wild the mind too faint the flesh; surrender,
Let the storm fade, the spirit fly;
Let stars be clear or let the night be tender,
But seal the eye.

Lie down, lie down; forever may the sun
Forget, and earth lie light,
And may the troubled spirit come on one
Use for the night.

(December 1937)

Philip Sparrow

Birdcalls wheeling overhead
Beat like wind upon my head;
Sharpened beaks of sparrows sup
On the heart I keep locked up
In its cage of blood and bone;
Where I walk to cry alone
Broken sparrows come to die

With uncomprehending eye
Staring innocent and blind;
Where I take my broken mind
Birds are broken on the wind;
Steel of winter and bad weather
Bites the heart and breaks the feather;
Starved in snow my ears have heard
The small, the bright, the suffering bird;
Hearing I have understood
How my life lets fall its blood
Softly in the sparrow note
Gold like blood along my throat,
How the sparrow speaks my word;
So we die my brother the bird.

(December 1937)

Spanish Harvest[25]

Here if the fields are mellow
And the sun kind, behold
The wheat-ear turning yellow
And the vine-leaf gold.

Who serve the corn and vine,
That men may eat
Gold grain and sunny wine,
Know both are sweet.

25. This is the first of several poems Davidman wrote about the Spanish Civil War (1936-1939), in which the Nationalists, with backing from fascist supporters in Germany and Italy, rebelled against the Republican government of Spain, who received aid from the Soviet Union and the International Brigades, composed of volunteers from Europe and the United States. Davidman and many other writers and intellectuals in the U.S., including the man who later became her first husband, William Lindsay Gresham, supported the Republicans.

We at a solemn meal
Devour with hungry breath
The little seeds of steel
And the grapes of death.

(January 1938)

Noel

The trumpet and triumphant horn
Cry upon the upper air;
Angelic harp and wing adorn
Arrival of a meteor.

Assuming mortal flesh and blood
He flares upon us for a sign;
Our hunger uses him for bread,
Our fever drinks him up for wine.

And nourished by the miracle
We turn our head from gain and loss
To spend a happy interval
Nailing his body to a cross.

(January 1938)

Benedick the Married Man[26]

I have a siren in my tongue,
A spider in my eye,
And I shall catch you with a song
And eat you till you die.

26. Here Davidman alludes to Benedick, the witty skeptic regarding romantic love
in William Shakespeare's *Much Ado about Nothing.*

I shall whistle you in from the farthest moon
That rings the ultimate star,
And lock you up in a spider room
With a cruel silken bar.

And I shall visit you at night
And lurk within your bed,
And you shall be my one delight
And wish that you were dead.

(January 1938)

Things Worth Saving

But I have not forgotten at all
The mapleblossom thick and small
And clustered on the branches like bees;
Or blossom on the chestnut trees
Whose flowers fall as lovely air
Moth-white upon the heavy air;
Or in a darkness growing green
The frail and wild geranium
Standing on a narrow stem
Like a soft star, and an airy star
Flowers called spring beauty. I have seen
Green shadows troubling the anemone
Colored like wind, I have seen violets
Yellow wearing brown veins like the wings of a bee,
Staring a million tiny times in summer's heart,
And the swift daffodils that smile and pass,
And the blue dayflower hovering like a dayfly
Two-winged and gold-eyed; and the flower that frets
Children and lovers till they pluck it apart.

And I have seen under an April sky
The little lily of the adder's tongue

Rising out of its two sweet spotted snakeleaves;
I have tasted on my tongue
The lilyleaf and the bitter black cherry,
The pointed privet leaf that leaves
Clean bitterness like hunger on the lips,
Green dandelion and the red rosehips,
The poppyseed and little elderberry.
I have gathered vineflower and spared the strawberry flower
And come again to eat wild strawberries
In the sweet month, June of the small wild roses;
And I have plucked wild iris in wet places.

I remember the sunset closing of buttercups
Bright and sleepy as tired children's faces.
And I have not forgotten honeysuckle
But I remember more the cruel thistle
And amaranthine pigweed and the cockle
And the purple-eyed burrs of burdock that followed me
 everywhere.
And I have found strayed myrtle to put in my hair
Under the last abandoned appleblossom
Planted strangely by some dead farmer and forgotten in the city.
Who has given perishing morning-glory pity
As I who opened my eyes upon it with the sun
And found the jewelweed within the wood?
Or who has loved and gathered goldenrod
Better than I who thought it curved like a woman
And made a queen of the goldenrod for my fairytale
Deep in the summer, when I lay at ease
After treeclimbing and my golden rambles,
Eating a grassblade, prickled by blackberry brambles.

This was my childhood under chestnut trees
Where ripened nuts came rattling down in a gale.
Bitter for eating but good to put on a string
And tie with a knot and use for a game and swing.

         (*January* 1938)

Prometheus[27]

My mind to me a viper's nest
And full of spotted poison is,
Where you may see the serpent crest
And you may hear the mortal hiss.

Whatever sweet the body knows
The thought has shriveled up with scorn,
And if my heart is like a rose,
Why then my mind is like a thorn,

And nailed on pinnacles of wind
The painful body lies at rest
While my own vulture of the mind
Fulfills its hunger from my breast.

(January 1938)

Tropic Night

Come in the shape of a dream, come like the wind,
Dead men, broken hands and foreheads turned to dust,
Give me the loveless mouth and the lean knees
Clasping my body;

Make a new glittering flesh of the grain of sand
Seeded so long in crannies of your bones,
Becloud your spirit in the flesh of clouds, dead men,
Come to my bed;

Come like a dream, and come like flowing water,
The live man with the forehead and hands of iron,

27. Prometheus was the Titan god who stole fire from heaven and gave it to human-kind. Once captured, he was bound to a stake on Mount Kaukasos where an eagle fed upon his ever-regenerating liver.

The lifted throat, the lifted eyes, the saint and demon,
The naked power;

Give me all beautiful bodies, the hawk-hearted,
Beast-hearted men, golden and fierce as tigers,
Cruel as the cold sharkmouth underseas,
Old wolf, young lion;

And let me carry jealousy into death
The voice like a god out of a living rock,
The living boy bearing so strange a mind,
So great a mind, so great a mind.

(February 1938)

To Anyone

If your face were stranger
Should I see it everywhere
And stumble into danger
For curling common hair

And a boy's emptiness
And a boy's mouth?
I should not need caress
The easy look of youth.

If you were made of silver
And not of lusty clay
I should not be your lover
Forever and a day.

(February 1938)

Damned Nuisance

To get your body for my delight
I would unstar the glistering night,
Disrobe the dawn;
With magic seated on my tongue
I'd set the world to spinning wrong
Or murder the sun.

To get your body for myself
I would turn toad or loathly elf
In secret caves,
And for each finger of your hand
I'd number all the silver sand
And chain the waves.

And I would do such horrid things
As never emperors or kings
On a peacock throne;
To kiss your eyelids while you slept
I'd do all miracles, except
Let you alone.

(*February* 1938)

Strength through Joy[28]

If you would have glory like a garment to cover your legs,
sit on your navel like a shirt of fire,
take from my hand the edgetool of destruction

28. This was Davidman's first poem to appear in *New Masses*, the semi-official magazine of the Communist Party of the United States of America (CPUSA). See *New Masses* 27 (April 5, 1938): 5. For more on her involvement with the CPUSA, see *Bone*, 2, 19, 31, 43, 80, 89-93, 95, 100-103, 109, 116-17, 120, and 137. See also Oliver Pilat, "Girl Communist [Joy Davidman]: An Intimate Story of Eight Years in the Party," *The New York Post*, Oct. 31; Nov. 1, 2, 3, 4, 6, 7, 8, 9, 10, 11, and 13, 1949.

and leave the cities of earth like rotten eggshells
staring sour and jagged at the barren moon;
and the parts of your body shall be glorious
partaking of my flesh. For I am he
the maker of honor, the hand bestowing judgment
seen in a cloud, the jaws of desolation,
begetter of dead men, eater of my sons,
and when any man is gnawed by the mouth of a cannon
I grow new teeth. I am filled with iron,
with fire and exhalations; I am magnificent,
honor the nails of my feet and the parings thereof
each being capable of killing. I am precious
and a treasure to women; honor then my knees
and the clasp of my thighs. And I will give you,
you, my dear children, my loving children, you
wearing my symbol on the fat of your arm
the beautiful moment, the moment of beautiful pain
with which you burst into flames; the high, the radiant
and honorable death. And when you die
be sure to use my name upon your lips
for your last word; this will be admirable
in you and me. I shall come
to set in your fallen flesh the roots of a tree
thorned and flowered with my name; your death shall be
a suitable decoration of gold at my breast
and I shall come bearing slaughter in the hand like bloodred berries
seeded with poison; glory for me,
glory, glory for me! and a bright crown of red berries.

(March 1938)

For Myself

Break the singing throat
and shatter the tongue;
what has been done in Spain
is not for song.

Though you can find a word
for any human stuff
whatever you make of Spain
is not enough.

Let the bright mouth be mute,
poet, be dumb;
make no smooth lines about
the Fascist bomb.   (*March* 1938)

If This Be Night

If this be night, then presently the sun;
If this is snowfall, flowers come in spring;
If this is storm, the wind will soon be done;
If this is silence, soon the bells will ring.

If this is rain, blue sky will follow after;
If anger, it shall come upon a sword;
And he in tears shall change his tears for laughter,
And he in chains shall make himself a lord.

Whoever lies in darkness shall possess
The earth below him and the sky above;
Whoever dies for folly, live for reason;
The color of the world be happiness,
The color of men's minds shall turn to love;
Consider this, and say, if this be treason.

(*April* 1938)

Promise

Three in a desert place,
Women, sisters, old,
Keep at the heart of space
Fire in eternal cold.

And when the fire burns white
Behold around the flames
Lean shapes that tread the night
Bearing kingly names.

And when the fire burns blue
In the black air behold
Things of thick flesh that spew
From a full mouth gold.

And when the fire burns red
The night shall pass away,
The sun shall raise his head,
The people shall have day.

(April 1938)

Weary Land

I shall now harden my heart like the rock
against all delicate faces of men and loves;
the moonlight softly coming shall be fruitless
fingering the barren stone. Nor by starlight
nor under the yellow eye of the sun shall these bones live
and breath be in them. I shall set up my heart
for a great rock in a desert of emptiness;
no rain, no wind, no grief shall strike it down.

Let me be only
the red rock cleft for seed to gather in,

the red rock and green splinters of the grass,
the flower out of the rock, the bitter flower
with strength for its root and bravery for petal.
Let me be the jagged breast of rock and the petal of the flower.

(May 1938)

These Foully Murdered

Be careful of these people who are dead;
touch their faces with love. Do not spread their names
staring in capitals for the admiring eye;
they are no decoration;
                              they are dead
your body has not felt their ways of dying
you have not counted the moments of their pain,
the club at the shoulder-joint, the frayed nerve-ending,
and the white bone visible, and the murdered brain.
What is the merry way of bombs to kill,
by what thin subtlety does blood desert the veins,
what is to die what unendurable stillness
to die; a man lays bare the cords of his throat; to sever
the fine sweet thread of nerve let fall through the spine;
the heart's fruit cut open, the eyes finished; to end the sky,
being desolation over trees and silence above clamor.
This is the shape of death and there shall be no speech
and there shall be no more little pictures in the skull.
You do not know the abominable savor of death
which they have eaten like bread. You will not go
under the earth where they lie hugging death to their bellies.

And though there is honor for them, you will not find it
using their names for a cheap wreath; and if honor
was not in their minds, but only the red flag
and the people, bruises, the cold, and the hunger, the people,
whips and scorpions, the slums, the cold and the hunger;

if this was in their mind; if pain was in their mind; to hold
green, sun, blue, rainbow and music cupped in two hands
and let the sword enter for the red flag

                              do not repay them
with dedications. Do not give them praise.
Say their names over once; Liebknecht and Luxemburg.[29]
The dead with names, Sacco and Vanzetti;[30]
the many dead without names; the dead in mud
who look up and see the earth wheel down upon them,
the dead in streets who look and see bombs
silver and growing large in the air; the fifty years dead
shot down in the strike; also those two days dead
shot in the strike; the dead unsuspecting
struck by a blow of the sky; the dead who knew
meeting bullets with bare teeth and laughter.

But now chiefly,
looking in the mirror, looking with bare teeth,
say to yourself the names and faces that will die tomorrow.

                                        (May 1938)

In Praise of Iron

Love only iron things;
Love no gold petal,
No silver pair of wings,
No precious metal.

29. Karl Liebknecht (1871-1919) achieved fame immediately after World War I by leading, with Rosa Luxemburg (1871-1919), the Spartacists in the German Revolution against the government of Friedrich Ebert. Both were arrested, and before they could be moved to a prison they were murdered.

30. Nicola Sacco (1891-1927) and Bartolomeo Vanzetti (1888-1927) were two Italian anarchist immigrants who were arrested for the murders of a factory paymaster and guard. In spite of the public outcry in support of their innocence during the seven-year case against them (1920-1927), both went to the electric chair on August 23, 1927.

A man of silver and gold
To put in your bed
Will be so brittle and cold
He will freeze you dead.

You are too hard a heart
For beauty's tooth;
He who would break you apart
Must come with truth.

Accept the iron hand
Stripped of the velvet glove,
Kiss it and understand
This is your love.

(*May* 1938)

Sacrament

Give me your body and your blood to eat
And I am nourished as no goddess was
Who upon airy mountains had her meat
Of nectar and the fine ambrosias.

Give me your heart for wine, your eyes for fire,
The strength for milk, for sober bread the brain,
And cram the glutton mouth of my desire
With all your body knows of joy and pain.

Inexorable I am; and I am love.
I shall use all your flesh; I shall not leave
Either the spirit or the skeleton.
Now bring that sword your body; swiftly bring
Your naked steel for my sweet offering
And you shall burn in me as in the sun.

(*May* 1938)

Imperative

I will possess fine things;
Silver and steel,
And yellow finger rings,
Good wine and meal.

I will own loveliness
Of cloud and fire
And I shall make my dress
Bright as desire.

I will have good treasures
Brought from north and south,
And songs, and subtle pleasures,
Your hands, your eyes, your mouth.   (May 1938)

To a Good Actor

Now never tell me that you are austere;
Speak not of chastity. You are not he
Cold-mouthed and cloistered up in modesty.
Assume your saintliness; yet you appear

As one who shall not with a fingertip
Touch me but that he shall be prey to fire;
Now do not softly muffle your desire.
I know your nostril; I can read your lip.

There is a hawk that sits within your breast,
A running stallion pounding in your blood;
You are compact of beast and bird and flame,
And in your private heart you nurse the nest
Of such a clamorous and scorpion brood
As all your good intentions will not tame.   (May 1938)

Genetrix[31]

I shall have the making of you in my hands,
I shall make you over again;
I shall breed your body out of the pain of my womb
and put my flesh with it to make it wise.
And you shall have again the shape of your head
and the strength crouching in the corners of your eyes.

I shall put your bones together, one by one,
and set your heart beating in the midst of all
and the mouth shall be you that plucks at my breast;
you will live in the eyesockets, and you shall be
a laughter, a small noise, a wordless happiness
closed in my arm, loving my breast and me.

These are your fingers I have joined together;
these are your hands that I have made with care,
these are your feet made new by my love.
Man, you are a new creature, dear and wild
with your new thoughts and your familiar hair,
and being my lover, you shall be my child.

(*June* 1938)

Postscript: But All I Want

... but all I want is the sense of your mouth
but all I want is the look of your mouth and eyes
but all I want is the hair on the back of your head
to run my finger over;

31. This poem was originally included in the manuscript of *Letter* but was removed
at the suggestion of Stephen Vincent Benét; see Davidson's letter to Benét of July
26, 1938, in *Bone*, 13. The poem appears in *Bone*, 10-11. The title is from the Latin stem
meaning "to beget."

your body the great and bare and splendid creation
come down upon me like the weight of god
descended upon me like the thunderbolt
eating me wholly

but all I want is your presence your possession
the shaft of fire the great agony the great beauty
the lifting up and using of my body
to give you pleasure;

I would embrace you with my hands and fingers
clasped across the strong bones of your spine
and feel the joints of your body with my fingers
and I would

and I would love you beloved who leave me here breathless
lying without knowledge of the muscles of your body
but all I want is the sun, but I want earthquake,
but all I want
all I want ...

(June 1938)

Tenson[32]

My pure and silver part,
My bloodless elf, the brain,
Sees with a fine disdain
That foolish beast, my heart.

Beast, you were made to bear;
Subdue yourself, be wise;
Constrain your savage eyes,
Discreetly bind your hair.

32. The French word *tenson* denotes a lyric poem of dispute in which two opponents
speak alternate stanzas, lines, or groups of lines, usually identical in structure.

Beast, you were made to weep;
Out of your hollow breast
A great noise of unrest
Cries and will not sleep.

Good ass, my heart, lie down;
Gently assume your load.
You shall have straw for food
And you shall have a crown

Of straw both white and black
To set about your ears,
And all your worldly years
Bear riders on your back.

This cruel and comrade breath
My heart has from my head
While both together tread
The bitter road to death.

(*June* 1938)

Artificers[33]

Cellini[34] made a drinking cup
So fine that from it no one drinks;
Fluted the gold and curled it up,
And set thereon a woman sphinx.

He gave her glitters for her eyes,
Tinseled her skin instead of fur,

---

33. This poem was originally included in the manuscript of *Letter* but was removed at the suggestion of Stephen Vincent Benét; see Davidson's letter to Benét of July 26, 1938, in *Bone*, 13. The poem appears in *Bone*, 6.

34. Benvenuto Cellini (1500-1571) was a Florentine sculptor, goldsmith, and writer. He is often remembered for his highly readable account of himself and his period in his autobiography.

Painted her mouth both warm and wise;
The gold is none too good for her.

I will take bronze and make your face,
Or I will carve you out of tree,
And what you have of fire and grace,
That shall you have eternally.

Cellini made his lover small
To grace a cardinal his meat;
But I will build you tall, so tall
The world shall froth about your feet,

And I will paint you on the sky
And set you shining in the air,
And men shall come to read your eye
Or guess the meanings of your hair,

And you shall admirably stand
For other loves, other times,
Gold and immortal from my hand;
All this I give you in my rhymes.

(*June* 1938)

What Song the Sirens

There was a fountain where a boy
Made a water-nymph his joy,
Kissing coiling under water
Took his fill of the fountain's daughter,
Till her flowing flesh and his
Went together in a kiss;
Now one body and one bone
These two make one carven stone;

She has drunk his body up
Like sweet liquor in a cup;
He has used her heart and head
Like good nourishment and bread;
Underneath her dappled water
He became the river's daughter,
And his bitter hands grew kind
With the art of womankind,
And the wisdom of her breast
Saved his soul from sharp unrest.
Some such way my love would do
Its little miracle on you;
Leave your iron and your pride,
Give you gentleness beside,
Medicine your bleeding grief
Softer than a mullein[35] leaf
Some such way my spirit slips
With your breath between your lips,
Leaves you arrogant and fine,
Mortal half and half divine,
Strong as thunder, swift as water;
At your heart the river's daughter.

(*June* 1938)

Pantheist

Every leaf upon the tree
is in soul akin to me.

Arrogantly leaf and I
fling ourselves upon the sky,

---

35. A plant typically with rosettes of greyish woolly leaves and tall erect racemes of flowers; in this case probably the yellow-flowered *Verbascum thapsus*.

59

find our bodies brought to earth
making winds the stuff of mirth;

flaunt the fine green of our youth
nibbled by the vermin tooth,

eat the sun and sicken on shade;
of one flesh we two are made.

No marvel if it come to pass
that my body shall be grass,

and to comfort you in life
you shall have the sod to wife,

and for pleasure when you're dead
I strike root above your head.

Every leaf upon the tree
will be rotten with you and me.[36]   (July 1938)

Daily Business

My blood said: let
this heart be loud
as voice of thunder
in a cloud;

my breath said: be
as small, as cool
as snow alighting
on a pool;

---

36. In the typescript of this poem Davidman indicates that it was written during
her stay at the MacDowell Colony in the summer of 1938. For more on the MacDowell
Colony, see Bone, 11-12, 14-15, 30, and 108, and http://www.macdowellcolony.org/.

then my bone spoke:
be now the drum,
beat betokening
kingdom come;

my spider mind
to speech was stirred,
being thus final
in a word:

arise and shout;
lie down and weep;
count yourself lucky
you end in sleep.

(July 1938)

Jacob and the Angel[37]

Within a hollow place
My angel soul and I
Locked in a hard embrace
Wrestle till we die.

But I will not be made
Slave of my better part
Or sell to my wise head
My idiot heart;

I will eat fire and snow,
And bleed and thrive,
And I will gladly know
I am alive;

37. The title alludes to the biblical story of Jacob wrestling with an angel. See Genesis 32:22-31. Davidman indicates that this poem was written during one of her stays at the MacDowell Colony.

And I shall let my soul
Take flight upon the wind;
Stuck in a narrow hole
Remain behind;

Endow with all my strength
Whatever worms have birth
When I am dead at length,
Out of this rotten earth.

(July 1938)

Flood

I and the water are not seen
as we come up from underground
turning the trees from brown to green,
eating the rocks without a sound;

I and the water are not felt
so nimbly do we lap at your lip,
and you have seen our snowflake melt
like steel upon your fingertip.

We are not loved, we are not known,
as nameless as the light of day;
use us until your thirst is gone
and what is left you throw away;

but you shall hear the thunder crack
and cry aloud our name again
when the water comes lisping back
at the doors and windowsills of men.

(August 1938)

First Lesson

If you being poet and the lover of pain
will come upon it softly; if you will walk
keeping your feet ungrimed and your head unwounded;
if you will hold your mind up for a mirror
to any empty shining of the air;
if you will have a game: despair, despair;
if you will mouth ghosts and the unimportant stuff of beauty;

you will not know
how the spirit of man cries at the coming in and going out.
You will not living feel the trap shut its jaws on your neck.
You will not be insecure; no one will devour you
and another thing you do not know is how to be alive.

Do not hope to fashion pain into a wreath
and have all comers stare at the light about your head;
pain is not subtle. It is common bread;
it is the common stone of every day,
the cracks in the pavement and the dirt thereof;
this is the true ache of humanity
and it will not set demons at your head and feet
but it will put hunger in your belly, cold
at your fingers' ends and dampness in the place of your lung.
Pain is no miracle. It is a thing
having weight and a round shape and a taste of its own.
Walk with the bums, pick it up from the pavement and put it in
    your mouth.

No agony
you stumble on in the dark of your spirit
will ever so wound you across the mouth and eyes
as the food glassed within the grocery store.
You will find ways your body has of being sore.
Neither shall demons of the mind nor ghosts
of your sweet loves nor the monotony of day upon day

grinding you between the upper and nether millstone
encompass your destruction. You shall be hurt
as simply as the rabbit by the hound's tooth.
Nor will they make a glory of you and splendidly lay you
bent backward heels to head on the altar stone;
the priest displaying your heart for the bright beaks of his gods.
You shall only be hurt.

Nor will they bring you
the nails, the crown of thorns, and the white garment,
and when you are dead you shall be very dead.

But this much you shall wear upon your head;
a thing called a headache contrived by hunger
not to be removed by the cup of coffee for five cents.
But this much you shall wear in your fingers: cold.
You will tramp on cobblestones and feel your feet aching.
You will ride all night homeless in subway trains
making sleep out of the brief roar between station and station.
You will know the rain but not as sweetness;
you will learn the snow
and watch it turn on your sleeve from silver to steel.
Each of your fingernails will be a separate nail
of the cold, of the nagging winter air.
And you will not find good words to say of all this
other than when your mouth burns: I am hungry;
other than in the doorway: I am frozen;
other than in the moment of your death: I suffer.

When you have come home from this, come again
to the clear air and the attitudes of your soul;
when you are set free and fed again;
if you will nibble beauty from the air
remember the broken face under the streetlight
the spoiled humanity the broken meats
this and this one hunting garbage in the streets;
remember the blind and multifarious stare

the city multiplied in eyes and each
eye bitten through its center by the worm of grief.
Having shared in these vulgarities of pain
you will not like your sweet soul much again,
you will not sleep but you will take your hands
and your tongue and your two lips and use them to serve an end;
you will use words;
                              refashion with your breath
the commonplaces of this life and death.

(August 1938)

For the Conveyor Belt

Little children I have walked with you every day;
unclosing our eyes in the first ringing of morning
you and I together have seen light weak and soiled
put fingers through the windowpane. I have eaten your bread;
your face and mine upon the trolley car
travel against the climbing sun. This is I
hanging from one strap with you and murdered at your side.
The gates of the factory open and shut. Wisdom
comes to children with the act of doing.
By such and such motions of your hands shall you learn wisdom.

And when the metal leaves your hand
it is a bolt. And going from your fellow
it is put with other metal shining and new;
and when all of you have taken it in your hands
it is a Ford car and this is wisdom
and we go out for lunch.

O now together
we sniff the air roasted with hot metal
and the sweet breath of air sent in by trees
stirs here and there but always over our heads;
we stand on tiptoe for the air;

together
child does your brain ache brother is your hand cramped
bent in the shape of the work of every day;
little children I have seen with your eyes
the rows of automobile parts the passage
swift of the conveyor belt the wisdom of this world.

Little children
what have they given you for that blue stare
with which first you fronted the ways of the world;
what have they given the curling of your fingers,
what have they given the sucking mouth for its mother's milk?
Child of my body and father of my body,
have they so shrewdly spelled for you weariness
that you will be the child and the old man
and nothing else; but westering see the sun
tell tales upon you that your hands are done
binding up for some hours the fractures of steel;
little children we will go out under the sky
and carrying homeward with us the smell of our sweat
we shall be made blessed by the returning bed.

Or else;
this too I have known;
I like you have burnt my weary brain
grassfire with whiskey; like a fire of seeds
scattered into nothingness that which will not arise.
I have used my hands for cruelty and the parts of my body for lust.
We have been foul together we have wakened together
wearily in the renewed morning; we have died together; what shall
    we do
They have broken our backs what shall we do
They have rotted our eyes with tear gas what shall we do
They have not given us enough bread or enough peace
they have dishonored us; what shall we do to them
when we are grown when we have grown to be men little children?

(August 1938)

66

Elegy for Garcia Lorca[38]

There was a man.
He opened his eyes and said
I perceived the dawn;
now he is dead.

He said: I perceived the dawn
walking upon the tops of the mountains,
setting its feet upon rooftops,
putting its fingers upon windowpanes to make their dust sparkle.
He said: I perceive the dawn arising in the heart of man.

They did not kill him for the dawn on mountains
because they have come to terms with mountaintops
out of whose gold and iron they can make a good thing.
They did not kill him because of many profitable rooftops.
They did not kill him in the name of dust; they love dust
and they would like his words to make it useful gold.
They killed him for the heart of man with which they can not come
      to terms.

He was born in the morning
and by nightfall he was a dead man;
he was reborn today
and tomorrow he will be born again;
he who is not dead will be reborn daily with the rising sun.

                        (*August* 1938)

38. First published in *Seven Poets in Search of an Answer*, ed. Thomas Yoseloff (New York: Bernard Ackerman, 1944), 34-35. Garcia Lorca (1896-1936) was a Spanish poet and playwright who was shot by a firing squad of fascist soldiers during the early days of the Spanish Civil War.

Office Windows[39]

This is about a thing you are about;
this poem is about the business of living
which you have set about;
                              you get up
leaving behind you the warm nest of night
the cavern in the bed the warm nest among vines
where you have lain dreaming all these hours
that you were small and the sun a good and simple thing;
dreaming of falling dreaming of taking a woman between your
        thighs
so many sorts of dream and each one labeled
ticket-to-your-mind by the psychiatrists;
and now the night laid by;
                              you must lay by
what you have not been and where you have not gone
fumbled at by the nightly snail's foot of the mind;
polish your face with running water into the clean mask of every
        day.

(This poem is about you, how you turn
from one side to the other to escape the morning,
awake reluctant; feel your eyelids burn
and wash them out with water)

so you get up in the morning so you refine
with pumice and with oil the crudities of your body;
so resurrection with the breakfast bacon
makes you a new and shining image set in the sun.

Come out and learn the pattern of the street
set naked and silent for daylight to climb upon;
the streetcar rails twist to your eyes sweet and colored silver;

39. First published in *Fantasy: A Literary Quarterly with an Emphasis on Poetry* 6, no. 3 (1939): 5-7.

there is bloom upon the cobblestones. Come out and see
how glorious from the feathers of archangels
the fire escapes are met together in the morning. Take so much time
to salute them as you need to reach the subway station.

(This is about your body under the overcoat
jammed in the rush hour with the shoulder against my back;
this is about your elbows and your neat eyelids,
the finicking contrivances of flesh and the universe
with which I am made familiar for an hour in the subway.)

O my brother
with our eyes we perceive the same squares of advertising;
the light and dark goes past the subway window;
so swiftly flicker the lights of day upon day
flash and the sun comes down bang and the moon rearisen
we ride in darkness flash and the sun rearisen
red light green light and riding in the subway
we have seen our lives chase each other past the subway windows.

But when you have reached your station where do you go;
what branching body of what street is made fertile
by your most individual presence; human thing
what office floor is amorous to your step
when you have taken your shoulder from my back
with your elbow deserted my shoulder-blade?

I do not know.
I cannot count the ways you have spent your life.
My fingers are not familiar with the creases of your rolltop desk.
How do I know when you have gone to the water cooler?
(but the look of the water in the dixie cup
blue and alive and creaming with the cold
and the water cold in your throat;
                                        the little steel
of the water drop left at the cup's rim: these
will you deny me brother?)

Permit me to share with you your drink of water
that I am mortal and the bands of flesh
tether me to thirst no less strictly than you,
though I shall never name all the ways you have spent your life.

Yield up to me the typewriter. Bring me the sewing-machine.
Lay the bookkeeper's columns of figures an offering before my feet.
(This poem is about you; do you know yourself?)

The little arrow on the neat shape of the dial
says the elevator is coming down
neatly from floor to floor; with measurable stops between;
and you shall be let out into what was sun
but now so thickened with the dust of the day
it is immolated like a body upon the car tracks,
sun of the late afternoon, skyscraper sun
angel dropping sidewise precarious upon the pavement
where the stuff of its body will be torn to rags by your coat and hat.
(Have you walked in this sunlight do you know your face?)
O the bright places to eat you will not go
the tiles you will not see shining, the painted dancers
slide all night upon the walls mocking humanity; but you
reunite your body with mine in the returning rush hour
 — The horses nibble each other, the cows rub flanks
and the light deer know each other warily with the tips of horns
but men ride in the subway and do not acknowledge each other.
This is the station where you mean to get out my brother.

The greatest accident of human life
the most comfortable illusion of mortal living
is what a man does with the space of evening
between his dinner and his sleep. How do I know?
How can I say with certainty where you have been
the cards spread in your hand the woman breasting your hand
the turn of light above the dancers; where
have you lain in Central Park upon grass or newspaper?
(But you have done all these things do you know your face?)

And when you are done writing your name in beer or water
with your fingertip upon the restaurant table
when you have heard the music come round again
and the horns perishing where they were born;
when you have seen the film come round again
the necessity of sleep is come upon you.

Do you dream
that you are falling down an endless flight of air
set without steps in the mockery of stars?
Do you dream that you are pursued by motor-cars?
Have you had dreams in which your house changed into a turtle
and . . .[40] but you were away you had gone walking
out in the sun in the undiscovered country
and you had gotten away into the clean fields?
But whether you dream this or another thing
you will be called back and with pain remake your morning face;
brother tell me why
sharer of weekly salary tell me why
fellow sufferer of the compulsions of humanity tell me why?

(*August 1938*)

Bierstube[41]

Though perfectness be come to dust,
spotted the throat of every flower,
funerary the end of lust,
how sweetly sit this perfect hour
beneath the table thigh to thigh,
secret and warm my love and I.

But time will part these lovers' knees
that kiss each other knob to knob;

40. The ellipses are in the original.
41. A German or German-style tavern or café.

time will make the finger freeze,
strip the flowering breast and rob
my flank; the hour will be through,
And there is nothing I can do.

(September 1938)

Jericho[42]

Seven times around the city wall;
And I will assail you with the cries of trumpets
And you will see your stony tower fall.

You are betrayed privily by the strumpet's
House in the market-place; by the scarlet thread
She lets fall at the window and ties to her bed.

You are betrayed most by your private heart
Which will set the city thronging with desires
Like a pointed cloud of arrows, like thick fires.

Frown out of your eyes and stand apart;
With insulting trumpets I shall call;
Not a stone shall lie untroubled in your wall.

I was in the heart of you last night;
Coming to shelter in the harlot's house
Between the sunset light and the half light;

By no warder was my coming stayed;
I walked your enemy. Quiet like a mouse
I stole upon your heart. You are betrayed.

(September 1938)

42. The title alludes to the biblical story of the walls of Jericho. See Joshua 6.

Rough Sonnets

I

What is he doing in her room this hour of night
Who is no more than a guess within her mirror,
Who is no more than a glitter in the corner,
Than a trick, than a contrivance of the moon and gloom;
What is his presence doing in her room
More than every day he does in her heart
Where he lives both the night and the daylight;

For whatever she does the air will thicken
With suggestions of him round about her head;
He will stand at the four posts of her bed,
At the four cardinal points of head and heart
And naked feet and hands; he will quicken
Her dreams with images. What is he doing
Tonight whom she invokes to her undoing?

II

She is ostentatious of her love.
Running to everyone: see how I am hurt,
Here is his name I continually repeat
Like slow drops of water dribbled upon my head,
Here is the unmistakable color of my blood;
Here are the wounds upon my hands and feet.
Examine my body, see it stripped upon the bed
And admire the marks made by love and loneliness.

Only to him she will not say anything
Nor reveal to him that she loves him, because she loves him
And will look at him smiling like a lie;
And seeing that her body is all one cry
Leaning forward to him across emptiness,
If he will not hear that he shall not hear anything.

III

One would think that she, feeling love stoop upon her
Like a striking bird; she, feeling her body wounded
And sickened by the talon; she, confounded
Past the bloody hell of all dishonor
Would cut the talon loose, get free of the biter;
Guard her softness against this merciless
Tooth of the contriver of distress;
Look for cloud or parapet to hide her;

But she will hug the creature in her arms,
Give it her breast to eat; she will lie down
Wearing the pain against her side in place of a lover,
Close around it and keep it warm, for she can see
Whatever else love is, it is kindness and company
And she does not wish to be alone.

IV

Nothing she could do would keep this moment
From breaking; nothing could save the glass bubble
Of this moment and his face across the table,
But they would be shattered by the hammer-stroke
Of the next moment falling from the clock,
She knew; his face and hand impermanent
Hovered a long age in the air but they would be gone
And recalling the ghost of them would be trouble.

But since the moment was excellently bright
She reflected that she need no longer care much
If the future made another such;
Then she herself broke the moment with laughter.

Nevertheless she was unhappy later that night
And for a considerable length of time thereafter.

V

"O love, magnificent and dreadful love"[43] —
He who had said this had no idea of her,
Who stood by mutely with her hands and her mind burning,
Who cautiously made words; talking of
Tinsel and a moonlight and a star;
While having said this and eaten he was satisfied.

But whenever he moved her eyes turning
Took her walking around the room behind him,
And she would walk on dusty roads to find him
Or walk tangling her fingers at his side;

She would not have known then what you were talking of
If you had been good enough to mention
This sorry passion and this sad confusion
By the fine and dreadful name of love.

(September 1938)

Spanish Landscape

Swallow, swallow, flying south,
bird with the iron wing, aeroplane,
bird gnawing with a buzzing mouth
into the milky spaces of the sky
over the level fields of the defenseless grain;

bomber when you come home at evening where do you leave your
    bombs,
eggs of the new dispensation; what nest of towns

43. This line appears in a poem by Gaspara Stampa (1523-1554), considered the most
famous female poet of the Italian Renaissance. The key passage is: "O love, magnificent
and dreadful love / At last consuming heart and brain." Davidman probably encoun-
tered the poem in William Rose Benét's *Moons of Grandeur: A Book of Poems* (New York:
George H. Doran Co., 1920).

have you hung your wings upon?
Bird with wide wings set motionless
in the shape of gliding upon the wind's crest,
where have you let your bombs down?

Evening brings the sheep bleating home
and the goats with sharp horns scattered by day upon the plain;
evening brings the bomber to the hangar
and the child running to his mother;
wine to the weary men; warmth to the sheep;
starlight and gentleness and sleep.
Evening brings the bomber without the bomb;
does it bring the child to his mother?

(September 1938)

In All Humility[44]

Now I rejoice that I am made of common earth;
I celebrate this double handful of the dust;
I would not have it anywhere forgotten
That I am child of no miraculous birth
And by no fabulous fathering begotten,
But by a man on woman in his lust.

The hands I use upon you are not more fine
Than any body of man and woman engendered;
To man's indignity they have surrendered
And do not wear the shape of the divine;
They are not the pointed wings of birds;
They are not the walking feet of spirits;
And the words I use are not divine words;
I speak to you with no unerring tongue.

44. First published in *Fantasy: A Literary Quarterly with an Emphasis on Poetry* 6, no. 4 (1940): 27.

Whatever be its graces and its merits
It will discover ways to do you wrong,
For my speech will stumble and you will not understand;
Misunderstanding to your hurt and mine
You will put forth your strength against my hand.

See now; my hands are broken by your love,
My body is good bread
Made and broken that you may taste thereof;
My breast is good to put beneath your head
As you would lay your forehead on the earth;
Whatever I may be worth
I shall enchant you with no gift of stars
And be no furious fire to harrow your flesh;
But you shall rise afresh
From my embrace to fight anew your ancient wars,
And by my arms made brave
Conquer for a little time the assaults of the grave
Before the returning sun shall see you dead.
Subdue your ambitious spirit to find in me
Reviving nourishment; accept my bed
As a perishable pleasure of mortality,
And love my earth, perceiving in my face
The natural comfort of the commonplace.

(September 1938)

Burnt Child

How innocent and how amazed
I put my hand into the fire;
I did not know destruction blazed;
I thought it was my heart's desire.

The flame licked up my silly skin,
Consumed my bravery and drove

Me mad; I threw my body in,
I burned my very bones with love.

The fire burned out; the embers died;
The ashes crumbled and I crept
Into a soothing place to hide,
And there for nights and days I slept,

And there I made my body whole
With medicine of sun and rain;
But still I wore upon my soul
The bitter cicatrice[45] of pain.

When upon guarded feet at last
Into the burning world I came
The second time, I saw there flashed
Across my path a second flame.

I know; I have been wisely burned;
I know what sweet device is here;
I taste the lesson I have learned
And I am stiff and sick with fear,

And this is not by my desire;
And yet for all that I can do
I give my body to the fire
A second time, for love of you.   (*September 1938*)

Notes on an Obsession

I
Never and never while the blood runs warm,
the bonehinge bends to order, the soft wet
sponge quivers in my head, am I likely to forget

---

45. The scar of a healed wound.

the shape of your head and the bending of your arm.

Having once seen you, how shall I undo
image of your image printed on my brain,
and the bitter thirsting and the long pain
of a life without you how shall I undo?

O terrible beauty; you with your wry mouth,
your wrists and your fingernails and thighs
and the desperate bravery in your eye.

To call the creature love might be a lie;
there is no kindness in it. This much truth:
I shall desire your body till I die.

II
Let me not lie about it; there are worse pains.
There is seeing your children shot before your face.
There is being buried alive in the shallow graves
Where afterward the torn sods heaved in vain.
There is gripping the bars and staring out at the rain
With fear cutting your belly like a knife.
There are many deaths and several sorts of life
That are much worse than what I feel for you;
And yet this loss is loss, this love hurts too.[46]

III
At the last hour the few important things
she kept firm hold of, had not much to do
with what she said and suffered, what he knew
or thought about it all; or even love.
When they marched her to the king of kings
it was not these that she was dreaming of.

46. This stanza also appears as the first nine lines in sonnet IV of the sequence to
C. S. Lewis that appears later in this volume.

She had outlived the agony of wonder
what he was really like inside his head,
forgotten the harsh nights and lonely bed
while the long meteors died without a trace
down the abyss of sky, and all her pains
forgotten, when the angel came to thresh
her spirit from her bones. One thing remains,
one arrow still may burn, while flesh is flesh;
the accidental beauty of his face.[47]   (*September* 1938?)

To Love and the Lover

There are no words simple and round in my hand
As the fact of you that I would put in words
Sweet as water, clean like new wooden boards.
There are no words having a slow and simple sound
Meaning you if I speak them. There is no sound
Which will make you so clearly for the beholder
As the simple turning of your shoulder
Or as your feet striking upon the ground.

I have learned subtleness, and I must unlearn it;
I have learned secretness; I must abjure it,
Break my private closet, shatter my locks;
To make your natural image for the world
I must be clumsy and honest like a child
Spelling with the simple shapes of building blocks.

(*October* 1938)

---

47. This is a slight variation on the sonnet form since it contains fifteen lines rather than the normal fourteen lines. These lines also appear as sonnet XVI in the sequence to Lewis.

Though Transitory[48]

This is a good thing to be young;
having the brightness laid along my skin
gold and the gold hair slightly

stirring with the lift of my arm; a good thing
having the clear brave whites of my eyes shining
and the eyes moving lightly.

And the backs of my hand are as smooth as a laurel leaf;
as the slippery stem of a water-lily leaf,
and the skin of my shoulder good to nuzzle with my mouth.

In the time of youth there is a sweet taste in speaking,
In this time I have gone walking,
taken the wind in my teeth;

gone upon the harsh pavement and beneath
the sweet whistle of the air and sun
and sunset filled with coolness.

Being young
it is a good thing to feel the joints of my body
swing upon each other with pure delight;

lie straight in bed and sleep well at night
and waking with clean lips taste the cold new air.
I like this waking better than happiness

which furs the body with sleep and keeps it warm;
I like my cold youth and the sting of wanting
and the pain knotted in my throat and the storm

48. First published in *Fantasy: A Literary Quarterly with an Emphasis on Poetry* 6, no. 4
(1940): 26-27.

of tears like easy silver that I give distress
and am free of it; wounded with a clean spear
and no canker; bleeding honest blood

brave and red and a pleasure to see; delight
tasting sharp and unexpected in my mouth
and pain like a strange spice; this is youth

that makes the suck of breath a fine thing
and the repetition of the pulse in the wrist
the tick of a fine clock.

And when I am hurt
youth is a shield to turn the blow and a good medicine
like a green leaf laid over aching eyes;

for I am never so bruised upon the mouth,
so betrayed into sickness that I cannot rise
tasting the morning; take the wind in my teeth
remade by the dear miracle of youth.

(October 1938)

Threat: There Is No Room in My Body

There is no room in my body
For myself and another;
The little place I live in
I share with no lover;

The passage in my throat
Is not so wide
It can use breath and food
And crying beside;

Within my guardian ribs
I make the world

In colors as it lives,
But no man's child;

One of us must make ready
To set his spirit free;
There is no room in my body
For you and me.

(October 1938)

Our Vegetable Love[49]

In this unreason
Suddenly I
Into sunlight frozen,
Congealed in the sky,

Perfect as leaves
Whose fine color
Makes of the trees
A light-bearer,

Stand immortal
Motionless, lest
Breathing a little
Murder blessedness.

(October 1938)

49. The title alludes to a line in Andrew Marvell's "To His Coy Mistress": "My vegetable love should grow / Vaster than empires, and more slow."

Ex Voto[50]

Not less under daylight than
under the night's
closed house of darkness;

not less in the city
making straight walls
than among the sweet seed of grasses;

whether by tongues and laughter
surrounded or in silence;
whether thick with eating

or clean of food
in the blank midnight;
not less in loneliness

than pleased by friends
do I remember your face
and the shape of your hands.

(October 1938)

High Yellow[51]

What tree are you grown from,
what flower from your mother's nipple come;

what leaf is your tight hair dancer?
How are you cut and carved and set in motion, satinwood,

---

50. The title refers to a votive offering to a saint or deity.

51. First published in *Fantasy: A Literary Quarterly with an Emphasis on Poetry* 7, no. 1 (1941): 21. This poem, along with "New Spiritual" and "So We Can Forget Our Troubles," appeared collectively under the title "Amateur Night in Harlem."

your knees turned on the lathe, your belly smoothed,
your round eyelids and your neck polished smooth?

What bird are you made from,
what wing made the shaking of your arm

and the rapid shifting of your feet;
what peacock feather eyed your teat?

But this is neither stem nor wing,
a human body poured in a gold skin;

but we would like to touch your flesh;
we would get pleasure from your touch,

with quick motions of our eyes
we possess the muscles of your thighs,

since in the clutter of living we have known
no body so beautiful and brown,

no laughter so entirely meant,
no dance so fine, no lust so innocent.

(November 1938)

Interpreter

My body is a bad tool;
I have not sharpened it.
It is a dry stick;
the weapon of a fool.

I use it to dig earth
and pry at rock;
and it will break,
a lever of no worth;

by it I cannot have
the good things I need;
it will not be glad,
it does not get me love.

By it I get pain;
if I discarded it
there would no longer sit
fever in my brain.

Yet this body I keep
since I can command
the engine of its hand
to take this pencil up,

crook its finger bone,
pick its words and write
in black line on white
my soul's immortal groan.

(November 1938)

Jews of No Man's Land[52]

We, stripped in this unmerciful year,
naked to the front and end of it, to the blast
two ways from the future and the past,
we despoiled of our houses; sold to the sky; here

Poland to the right and to the left
Sudetenland; snarled at by two frontiers; Jew
Jewess and Jew-baby; the blue
sky for our cover patched by gasoline tins; bereft

52. First published in New Republic 99 (July 5, 1939): 248.

of the decent pillow and the mouth to mouth
in a good bed, in a tight house, the rain locked outside;
bearing our children under the thistle-stalk; dried
by weather; gnawed by the wind's mouth;

bearing our children in the dry ditch, between the winter's
slide of ice upon us and the autumn's rain;
wearing our good days tattered on our skin
in the shape of old clothes; given to the hunter's

shot and bullet, fair game in a dry meadow,
foodless, without bread, without body, we Jews
houseless, tongueless, without value, without use;
we are here; remember us; we dwindle to shadow,

we break our teeth on the hard winter; ghost
is our substance and the flesh of our hands; water
is the meaning of our words. Our tongues are bitter.
Our words run like melting ice. Our speech is dust.

You who pity us, you who are troubled by our names,
you who lie awake with your skin full of meat and
comfort held closely inside your hand,
you who look at us out of the warm rooms;

hold hard to your good thing that you may not lose.
Thus and thus it was with us; the same bread,
white and smelling warm; the bed
such as you have it and the ceiling above it;

lest the same come upon you in another country,
under another side of the sky, and you
fall useless into this nothing, and you
shiver naked peeled of your plenty,

learn how desolation was made for us!
Now we sit unhoused upon the ground,

our backs bent for warmth; the land
empty and the emptiness of sky over us;

daily we ask the question; is it bright,
is the gold face of the sun upon it, will it smile,
will it be kind and naked upon us or do we feel,
clouding the light and multiplying the light,

the round drop of rain that we have no room for
in our flesh worn and sweetened with rain;
will we have rain to eat; upon our chin
the dribble of the rain running over?

Learn how we were brought to this desolation,
how we were betrayed by our sleep and our
pleasant customs and peace and by the striking hour
lest it be done to each of you in your nation!

(November 1938)

Candles for a Lady

Set angels at your head and feet
And pennies on your eyelids; set
A stone to guard you from the heat,
A turf to keep you from the wet.

Here you lie as a lady should,
Toes turned up in her narrow bower;
Set a lock upon your blood
Lest it should ever make a flower;

Your heart shall be safe as you would have it,
Your honor clean as silver swords,
While your body and bones inhabit
These incorruptible four boards.

(December 1938)

With Your Meals

Water has no color, it is not
Silver or gold or peacock color, it is
Made changing with the changing light
As the daylight crawls to dark or bright;
Cold water is like silk, and water hot
Is an invisible serpent with a hiss
Out of its mouth like a white feather.
                              This
Is the power that plain water has
More than bloody wine or fruit in summer;
It is a kiss given to any comer,
It is a sweet taste on any man's tongue,
Good to put on your hands and caress your eyes
And roll your body in; and water is
Loved by all men like a common song.

                                        (December 1938)

Letter to a Comrade (1938)

Letter to a Comrade
(to Ellen Weinberg)[1]

Leaving New York, leaving the triple rivers[2]
netted in ships; turn again,
wanderer, turn the eyes homeward. Remember the city
settled in the eastward sky stiff with towers
crested and curved in the tight circle of home
cupped excellently in the sky. Possess understanding;
see this is your heart, turn and perceive these towers
sprung from the syllables of your mouth, this iron this crowding
and lighted fury of the trains emerging
out of the roaring tunnels of your veins.
These wings are birds born of the thoughts in your brain
the thick blue crowding of pigeonwings upon
towers belabored by the sun.
Feel your arms shoot and feather from the shoulder
into the skill of gulls overhead and over
steel and the bridges; tread softly under
footsoles the small dust filled with sparrows.

---

1. Ellen Weinberg and Davidman were fellow contributors to New Masses, the semi-official magazine of the Communist Party of the United States of America (CPUSA).
    2. The Hudson, Harlem, and East Rivers.

Letter to a Comrade (New Haven: Yale University Press, 1938) was published in November 1938.

This is the thought of your brain made jagged
into a city and the thought of other men, the various pleading
multilingual noise of seawhistles
comes out of the whole world under these bridges into the mind.

Turn comrade once
for you will never find elsewhere the aching eyes
and the familiar pain marked on the lips of men
but grief written hieroglyphic upon hostile foreheads.
Here remain the brothers of your heart, salute them;
here are the picket lines and the bright jangle
of children fighting, the glitter of streets, the houses in windrows,
here also the broken stairs and the fire and the rat
and here the impenetrable sheen of office windows;
but also you shall find here understanding for your speech
among many of the same flesh as your flesh
spoiled by the same poison. Forever
here are the beauty and pain fit for your eyes therefore turn them
        wanderer
finally from a hill at the edge of Jersey,
before departing salute your city
left hanging behind over waters.

II.
Comrade, go through the flatlands and the pallid country,
the reeds and marshes and the tar-paper bungalows
set in a row and with roofs shingled in two blended colors,
the bastard towns conceived in dirt. Go further,
go a day's journey to the other America,
breasted and milky earth, made of fruits and fat hills,
breeding woodchucks, hearing the bark of foxes. This is a land
divided between the buckwheat and the wheat,
white and green with the flowering, gold with rewards in autumn,
milky with breathing cattle; and the Susquehanna
feeds brown rainwater to the rooted corn,
slips gently over mountains, spreads thin to the sun;
steams vaporous in the air, climbs into cloud, comes gently

pressing its flanks against the flanks of mountains,
closes the valley from the sky and falls in rain;
so to the corn again.

Fifty miles to the south
it is known, the pulpy flesh of men makes war upon coal in
      the mines
and grapples with iron. In these pastures
there are no stones, there are no enmities.
Tender earth turns easily under the plow,
fecund under the male blade of the plow,
seeded and starred with young blades, later thick and singing
and the wind moves in the wheat like many snakes.
Clotted on furry stems in the hedge
sweetly the blackberries darken. The land loves its men.

The ruddy flesh of men grows out of red soil
and eats it, tasting new grain,
nipping the new kernel of the wheat with teeth
edged and hungry against the milk of the kernel.
These are the enjoyers of the earth, who feel
in their forking limbs, in the forking bones of their hands
and their feet, in the fibers of their hands
and feet, how the deep root goes down
forking in many branches, clenched on the guts of the earth.
They wear the earth in the creases of their hands.

How shall you speak the speech of these men how meet them
how read the meanings in their eyes how find them
how come to an understanding with their eyes?
Their tongues are heavy with an elder language
the slow tune of the water seeping among roots and of the
grass-blade creeping upward and of the
ripened apples falling softly among grasses.
How shall you speak to them, comrade, flesh of metal and jangling,
      quick flesh of the city?

But these
love the richness of life, desire food and sweet clothing,
the noise of strong children, the dazzle and knowledge of travel,
health and a roof and walls; these have a need of some love
and a little rest, like a sweet seed on the tongue, to savor before death.
Desire of your desire, beat in the heart like your heartbeat;
the bony knuckle bent with the selfsame tendon
and the bodies making love with familiar gestures;
and the bodies starving, seen behind the wried mouth
hidden in strangers sits our brother the skeleton
and all men grin alike.
These are made and jointed with old flesh and fed with blood
and they are beset, they dwindle, they perish, they pass;
the flesh of hogs is less than corn and the corn goes to waste;
the milk of cattle is less than the price of grain;
the yellow apples rot making many flies dizzy with drunkenness.
The women of the farmers spread empty beds with clean linen
for strangers, for the casual money of strangers.

Say then to these, there is no miracle of help
fixed in the stars, there is no magic, no savior
smiling in blatant ink on election posters;
only the strength of men, only the twigs bound together
invent the faggot, only the eyes that go seeking
find help in brother eyes. Say only
the spirit of men builds bridges of the spirit,
the hands of men contrive united splendors,
the need of men shall awaken thunderous answers;
and so fall silent. Leave silence among them. They will not have
     listened
to your words or being diverted with lies will not understand you;
they are easily befooled, soon betrayed; they have not yet come
clutching at wheatstraws, upon the end of disaster,
the bloody ultimate ruin, the wise destruction
immitigable strength.
Leave them their precious grain, the useless fruitage,
the money dribbling from their hands, the land

sucked from beneath their feet by the mouth more greedy than
    earthquake
of the blind worm of the age. Leave thought among them,
say to them your word and leave the word among them and leave
    them.

III.
Go wandering northward on the adventurers' track
who with fringed feet combed the Canadian dark
misguided by stars, misled by the polar star;
parceling their flesh among fields.
Here have their sprinkled heirs forgotten French laughter
stiffened upon the worn mouth puckered sourer
than tidal fields; and every whisper
makes war on brother whisper. Here divided
men have no voice more than the muted wave
unending on the shores.

And here the narrow moaning the little wave
rises divided between the ripple and ripple
the land divided by the arms of sea,
the tongues of land divided by the stream,
the farm divided by the tide; advancing
the moon, advancing and retreating, stripes water
with in and out; mutely the tide
cleaves the sand between wet and dry.
Here whispers lonely breath here find humility
marked on the map, written in the towns with saints' names
by the thin rivers and the stink of fish
and the yellow bricks of the true church; pray for us sinners,
pray for us now and at the hour of our death;

but not
that we being men rebuke this incarnation
and the wise ape in the mind; but not
that we are indolent and proud in flesh; but pray for us
pray for us; we sons of the French adventurers

salt and dry codfish beside a salty stream
here with no buyers; here our bread
stands to the flies; here our children
have no teeth, live on the thin flesh of fishes
and the pallid taste of Christmas berries plucked by the roadside
while waiting for the cars and money of tourists;
and because we have no teeth in our heads with which to bite
therefore priest pray for us, you sitting in the house of yellow bricks
which we have made beside the church of yellow bricks
which we have built and made bright with decorations of metal
and three white saints, and which we have given a tower
sheeted with tin, and of which we are proud because it is fine.

Priest give us good words and make intercession
to the Virgin that she may make intercession
since now every hour is the hour of our death.

IV.
Wanderer ending eastward
the spine of the eastern mountains trails to nothing
the tide runs outward eastward into nothing
the narrow fences of farmland dwindle eastward
only the sea remains. Nothing remains.

This is the land's end;
scream on the wind cormorant come cormorant
the sharp beak splitting the fish come seagull
come the small tern wheeling about land's end
and the crane stirring thin waters with feet of blue glass
feathering the wind and lonely upon the ocean;
come birdcry here is the heart here is the heart's cry, answer
along the ultimate and starving beaches
birdcry the voice of men.

And the children
go past on the wind crying in small voices
unheard blown seaward, shrill birdvoice of the children

buy this buy this, and the small claws of children
shaking a handful of green peas.
How shall this question be answered,
comrade, what strength shall repair this desolation
what shape of words what syllable bring courage
speak the united heart of men, unless birdcry
stringing long echoes on the empty air,
futile birdcry blown off the end of the world.

Here to the sea's edge, to the salt and bitter water,
descend the narrow birches left naked by fires,
the birch most tender and human flesh of all trees
reduced to essential bones of destruction; ah they are dead,
the white birch is dead and never again
puts forth the silver underside of leaves on the wind
or springtime tassels of the birch. They are dead,
the white trees, human birches; who shall call them
to lift the slaughtered branches upon the sky,
the murdered root to rise again by the sea's edge
at the world's end.

Only remember,
wanderer, under the murdered and slender trees
white bodies given over to slaughter, remember
only the fireweed, comrade, the glory in burnt places,
the sharply colored torchbearers, the new warriors,
the green and flowery resurrection, the fireweed
marching over burnt hills down to the sea's edge. Remember
resurrection riot among the roots of the birches, resurrection
out of the white and black bones of burnt trees, resurrection.
    Remember
with what a brave necessity the fireweed
answers birdcry down the desolate beaches
speaks to the aimless wind the heart's red syllable,
blooms on our bones. Let the fireweed answer,
comrade, and so we may lie quiet in our graves.

(*September* 1937)

To the Virgins[3]

Whatever arrow pierce the side
Or what confusion wring the mind,
Cherish the silver grin of pride
To stiffen your mouth in a whistling wind.

Love will devise you tricks of pain
Like fires, and gentleness a curse;
Never transcend the armored brain,
Never let in the universe.

Who lose their weapon find a wolf;
Who conquer wear a jagged wreath;
Therefore be guided; love yourself
And show the pleasant world your teeth.

(April 1937)

Crocea Mors[4]

Name of a sword: golden death,
golden, swoop over me, let the clear blood golden
fatten the earth, let the cruel wing go over
immemorial, and quietude succeeds
and steep innumerable intervals of reeds
slant upward from my eyes against the sky
sharpened with sunset yellow as any sword;
but wearily wearily the ascending bird
now darkens on the sky and wheeling
wing and wing over, lifting wing and wing,

3. The title alludes to "To the Virgins to Make Much of Time" by Robert Herrick (1591-1674).

4. *Crocea Mors* is Latin for "yellow death" and was the name given to Julius Caesar's sword, according to legends written down by Geoffrey of Monmouth (c. 1100-1154).

the sky wheels down its admirable crash of gold,
the sword wears blood.

Life let out
remain forever lost; no more than the moon drinking water
ever allow the wantoning blood return,
only lie quiet like the spilled golden moon
left in the sea forever. So torn
float glistering on air, so pass the spirit,
the pain so melt, confusion so dissolve,
so quietly among the water and reeds
under forgotten sunlight perish; so come
ultimately to quietude, so die.

(March 1937)

Spartacus 1938[5]

Thaelmann is buried under the peat bog,
under the rain, under the tufted grass.

He is buried under crisscross tracks of birdfeet
made all day by the moorhens as they pass.
He lies below the feet of prisoners
come all day from the concentration camp;
the lean march iris and the angled sedge
set their roots in grey and green water;
Thaelmann lies where the shovel's edge
crisscross cuts peat all day long
and the night smooths it over with water.

---

5. Spartacus (109-71 BC) was a Thracian gladiator and, along with several others, led the Third Servile War, a major rebellion against the Roman Republic. Davidman had dedicated the entire volume of *Letter to a Comrade* "To Ernst Thaelmann who will not know." Thaelmann (1886-1944), born in Hamburg, Germany, helped form the German Communist Party in 1920. A fierce anti-fascist, he publicly opposed Nazism, was arrested by the Gestapo in 1933, and was executed in Buchenwald concentration camp on August 18, 1944. The poem was first published in *New Masses* 27 (May 24, 1938): 19.

But Thaelmann is buried under Moabit[6]
lying living in the heavy stone.

When Romans killed Spartacus the gladiator
they did not put him under earth alone;
along the Roman road they set a cross,
a little way beyond another cross,
so for some miles, and every cross a man;
so the tall gladiators on the Roman road
blackened until the Roman flocks of crows
turned from the new corn in the spring.

This was done to Spartacus and the moneyless men
in the name of sweet peace, order and tranquility,
in the name of large lands belonging to one man,
the name of grain brought from Egypt to give the poor,
in the name of the rich man's house, the name of his sleep
and the fat ancestral spirits of his gods.
This was done in the name of the smoke on altars.
Spartacus being a slave was beaten with rods.
And the slave lives in the ergastulum[7]
and the slave lies chained to the outer door,
and the slave wears away the palms of his hands
working for the Roman state. Spartacus
lies with his heart buried at the foot of the whipping post.

(But Thaelmann is held in Moabit,
the door is locked, the key is lost, the cause is lost.)

The prisoners from the concentration camp
leave wet footmarks on the rainy moor.
They never had a key to open the door,
and when they leave, they leave by the back door of a bullet,

6. Moabit was a notorious Nazi detention and prison center in the inner city locale of the same name within Berlin.

7. An *ergastulum* was a Roman building where dangerous slaves were held in chains and other prisoners were punished.

the coffin sent home with an official seal;
but the prisoner shall set his heel
into firm earth, but he shall stand firm,
but he shall live by the lean gun
and he shall earn his death like honest bread
and there shall be bread. And this shall be
in our lifetime, in our bitter lifetime, Thaelmann.
The grass shall sleep upon the moor.

Assault the door, break down the door, break open the door.

(*March* 1938)

The Princess in the Ivory Tower

The Prince's voice, faint at the edge of sunlight,
where the clear sun leans backward from the night,
thin as a bird, faint as the fading air:

Rapunzel, Rapunzel,
let down your golden hair,

and I will climb up to the height of heaven,
and I will let the wind blow over my shoulder,
and I will let the stars drift through my hands,
coming to the magic house, the ivory chamber,
coming into the circle of dreams and drowning mist,
and wind will blow out both the witch's eyes.

Rapunzel,
let down your golden hair,

make a ladder for me to enter heaven,
make a ladder for me to dally with the stars,
make a stairway through the dizzy air.

There shall be no root upon the earth for my stair
and I shall sway between the sun and moon
and all the merry stars shall ring in tune
when I come in, when I come to the ivory room.

Let down your hair, let down your golden hair,
that I may be free from the murder at my foot,
that I may be free from the truth upon my eyes,
that I may be free from the worm at my heart's root.

(January 1938)

Twentieth-Century Americanism

Lies have been told about this American blood
making it seem like laughter or like some animal
couched with a golden throat in the desert. Our roots
push apart the bones of an Indian's skull. Arrowheads
strike fire and flint sparks out of us. These lies,
these Indian rivers, these arrowroot sweet waters
seething in the blue flag. We have not drunk these rivers,
we have not chewed and eaten this earth. These ghosts
do not walk in our veins with painted feet.

Come now all Americans
kiss and accept your city, the harsh mother,
New York, the clamor, the sweat, the heart of brown land,
the gold heart and the stone heart, the beast of American blood,
the cat stretching out before a borrowed fire
beside the steam heat, in apartment houses.

We are not the dark cheekbone of the Indian
and there are no painted feathers for our killing
which happens grimly, beside clapboard and raw steel.
We are not the stone ribs underneath Manhattan
but we come and go swiftly in the sick lights of subways;

men with narrow shoulders, children and women,
Italians, Jews, Greeks, Poles, and even Anglo-Saxons
all worn down to the thin common coin of the city.
And our minds are made after new electric models
and we have no proud ancestors.

                                          (Lost, lost
the deerskin heritage, the pioneer musket,
barn dance, corn harvest, breakers of new soil.
Lost the great night and thin assertive song
up from the campfire, lynxes drinking the Hudson,
bobcat in Westchester. What fish swim Manhattan,
what clean and naked rivers? lost and lost
the homespun and the patchwork quilt, the bread
risen in the home oven and smelling new.
Do not claim this for us. We have the radio.
We have the cat and the tame fire.)

                                          Beside
the bedroom window long trains ride,
the harsh lights come and go outside.

And our minds
and the minds of our children. Give us the World Series,
the ballplayer with thick nostrils and the loose jaw
hanging heavily from a piece of chewing gum,
and when the baseball is over give us no time;
fill our mind with the Rose Bowl and Yale and Notre Dame
leaving no time for thought between the baseball and football
     seasons.
Feed us music to rot the nerves, make us twitch with music,
burrow with music beneath the comfortless brain and beneath
the aching heart and the worn heart and beneath
the honest gut and rot the gut with music
in the snake of nerve that sits in the knee reflexes,
wriggle in the dust with the snake's belly. All night
delight us with the yellow screaming of sound.

And give us
the smile, the glitter of rich houses, the glitter,
porcelain teeth and skin smoothed by diffused lighting,
(skin-cream, face-food, oil of Peruvian turtles
bright and grinning out of all the subway advertisements)
the dark movie house and old cigarette smoke
and the knee of the stranger sitting in the next chair.
If you close our burlesque houses, we will reopen them
and watch twelve hours long the one crude smile
and the same silk uncover the same thigh.

And from the film
borne home to bed with the familiar wife
weary and good, and burrowing into night
into her breast with the blind face of a child;
out from the bed to the familiar daylight
the invoice the slick glass desktop the worn counter
and madam these goods guaranteed not to stretch.
Borne from the bed to sewing machines, taxis, and the building
        trades,
and if you wear a pencil behind your ear long enough you don't
        even feel it,
just like eyeglasses. And we go home at night
bearing in two hands like the image of god
the dear shelter, the clothing, the bright fine food.
And daily, daily, we expend our blood.

Give us this day our daily bread.
Give the pillow the aching head,
give Harlem midnight the hot bed.

Let not the trespass keep us from
the clean new streets of kingdom come.
Forgive the sin, forgive the slum.

But when summer comes
we will bathe in the city waters, pronounced free of sewage

only the doctors who swam there came down with a rash.
And in winter we will go skating in Central Park
being sorry for the animals who live in cages,
and the trees will be blue. And the towers will look blue on the
      snow,
the wet fine street will shine like a salmon's back.
And we shall see spring bloom upon the tops of skyscrapers.
We shall be happy. We shall buy silk and new ties
walking in the sun past bright stone. This is New York,
our city; a kind place to live in; bountiful; our city
envied by the world and by the young in lonely places.
We have the bright-lights, the bridges, the Yankee Stadium
and if we are not contented then we should be
and if we are discontented we do not know it,
and anyhow it always has been this way.

(May 1938)

Submarine

Water ringing like a bell
Curls the sunlight in its shell
Of a sea-worm hardly seen,
Long and luminously green.
Days that flare and nights that twinkle
Pass upon the sky to sprinkle
Gold and silver casually
On the serpentining sea.
Under hollow water I
Watch the bright and watery sky
Where a sun appears to swim;
Little fishes follow him,
And contemplate on wriggling tails
Each small perfection of their scales.
Crabs have feathers on their eyes;
This one spreads them out and lies

Underneath a flickering fin,
Sucking all the ocean in.
Round and round me go the fish
With a contemptuous silver swish,
Watching superciliously
The hermit crabs walk over me,
Each a spider, thin and black,
With a snail's house on his back.
Seaweed flowers to my hands
Out of variable sands
Where silkily and wetly slide
Purple shells with whelks inside.
Nothing in the sleepy sea
Complacent is as whelks can be,
So blissfully they eat and drink;
They do not talk, and if they think
Such lordly purple thoughts are those
Ocean imperially glows
Around each whelk become a star.
Marble all their faces are,
Benevolent and shiny slabs.
The sensitive and poet crabs,
Jointed, Japanese and frail,
Come and nibble a whelk's tail.
By this small symbolism see
Each great man suffers from a flea;
Whelks are statesmen in the sea.

(March 1936)

Prayer against Indifference[8]

When wars and ruined men shall cease
To vex my body's house of peace,
And bloody children lying dead
Let me lie softly in my bed
To nurse a whole and sacred skin,
Break roof and let the bomb come in.

Knock music at the templed skull
And say the world is beautiful,
But never let the dweller lock
Its house against another knock;
Never shut out the gun, the scream,
Never lie blind within a dream.

Within these walls the brain shall sit
And chew on life surrounding it;
Eat the soft sunlight hour and then
The bitter taste of bleeding men;
But never underneath the sun
Shall it forget the scream, the gun.

Let me have eyes I need not shut;
Let me have truth at my tongue's root;
Let courage and the brain command
The honest fingers of my hand;
And when I wait to save my skin
Break roof and let my death come in.

(December 1937)

8. First published in *New Masses* 28 (August 9, 1938): 17.

I the Philosopher

It has befallen me to see a thief
With a lovely body crucified; a perfect matter, deserving
    contemplation;
A pleasure edged bitterly; the flux of things,
The conscious spirit, or the eddying star,
The tangle of air and empty hollows of time
Knotted into being, can never arrange a pattern
Of rock or tree, of subtlety of tree
Spun greenly, of the barbarian rectitude of rock,
So fine as the serpentining flesh and mere two lines
Of crucifixion. How the willow flesh
Grows keen and admirable; naked
The twig, peeled white and twisted, stingingly helpless;
How every accidental bone and tendon
Serves a divine order; how clearly the harpstring cords of armpits
Swoop out, how musically sweetened ring with pain.

The slave takes three days dying, no longer lovely
Than one day and the following mist that abandons him
Black insult on the dawn; for presently bloodily wrenching
Pain crammed in a swollen mouth corrupts him; no longer
The early heroic impossibilities of the body,
No longer the virginal touch or delicate passing wingtip
And first sweet feathers of pain; so briefly go the graces,
And all his agonizing fires of perfection
Die pitiful as the brittle claws of dead birds.

Loveliness tickles the brain
And faint fans of nerve-endings in the skin,
Blunted by sunlight recurring obscene with flies.
We leave the slave. White fungus threads of thought
Drain him in the mooned and planetary spaces of the mind.
For what profound or starry, what whirling spheres,
Rings and celestial candles, what coruscations,[9] what fluid

9. Vibrating or quivering flashes of light.

Convoluted and ancient chaos must bend down
To make the quaint sinews of a man and nail him
Beautifully on a cross, and make my eyes,
My speculating eyes, my tremulous presence,
All for providing a lovely sharpened moment
In the long universe; unless for nothing
While still this jewel consummation rewards the womb
Of all blind ages. This is a miracle.

(April 1937)

Necrophile

These loves are buried under the heavy wind.
Sand trails upon them, empty bodies
Burned in the sun to outcast sand, a rubble
Of aching desert, futile swords and potsherds
Broken in whispering dust. Processionally
The shape of men, lifting great arms, the rippling of arms,
Falls into death. The bleeding discords
Become predestinate music; brutal flesh
Grows memorable by death and resurrection
Into the imperishable toy of history.

Glass may be stricken with music,
Sing like a cricket shrilly; then escaping
Sift sand between fingers.
From trickling dust arisen they will come
Into the significant fabric of my body.
I am contrived out of drifting ghosts; I am fed
On the great pride of Egypt, the armored snake
And sacred beetle, the jewel Scarabaeus[10]
Upon imperial foreheads; the angular limbs, the hawks

10. The sacred scarab of ancient Egypt, found in many paintings and pieces of jewelry, is a dung beetle.

Hieratically smiling wisdom; quiet Pharaohs,
Dark flesh and bright enamel; a thin mouth
Stopped with a bitter dust of spices.

These
In gold beatitude, with the violent head of Akhnaton[11]
Wry and human, shrivel in priestly linens
Drawn tight against the tooth of the jackal
Anubis,[12] among the pale eyes of the dead.

I suck bodily at desire;
Nations of broken clay, Sumer[13] and Akkad,[14]
The harsh virility of stone-bearded kings,
Stone Sargon,[15] membered like the bull,
Great scrolled stone, muscles and eyes of stone,
And godlike, eyed like the blind rock;
Loved also by Ishtar[16] and gods, drinkers of blood,
Squat Assyrians on the sun-dried ziggurats;[17]
Loved by the warm female moon, Ishtar, the cone
Set upon the earth between two rivers.

Tigris and Euphrates,
The yellow crawling beast, the perilous river,

11. A pharaoh of the eighteenth dynasty of Egypt who ruled for seventeen years, dying sometime between 1336 and 1334 BC. Historically he is noted for abandoning traditional Egyptian polytheism and introducing worship centered on the Aten. Some suggest he was the first monotheist, perhaps influenced by Moses or Joseph.

12. Jackal-headed god of the afterlife in ancient Egypt.

13. Sumer was the site of the earliest known civilization, located in the southernmost region between the Tigris and Euphrates rivers, an area today that is southern Iraq from around Baghdad to the Persian Gulf.

14. Akkad, the northernmost part of the Babylonian civilization, was a region in what is now central Iraq, located roughly in the area where the Tigris and Euphrates rivers are closest to each other.

15. Sargon the Great was the Akkadian emperor famous for his conquest of the Sumerian city-states in the twenty-third and twenty-second centuries BC.

16. Ishtar was the Akkadian goddess of fertility, love, war, and sex.

17. Staged towers of pyramid form in which each successive storey is smaller than that below it, so as to leave a terrace all round.

The rivers yellow as baked clay, together
Like the forked loins of a man, engender
Bearded and curled bulls, flat and stony lions,
Until repeated nations tread
Harsh cuneiform in the broken earth.

After such tortuous passion the clear gods
Flare upon me; immemorial Apollo[18]
In delicate flesh a precious substance of silver,
A thin wire sounding, walks in the curving sky;
The rank and burning goat, a dreadful ardor
Clasped closer than flesh to the spirit, called Pan,[19]
Lies in the night; all these are dead,
Cold at the core of the planet, lost upon air,
Spiraled into vapor, curled out and lengthening, blown
Subtler than wind; ineluctable, dragon destruction
Eats up the sun; these are dead,
And pass with the dry ash of many Greeks, Themistocles[20]
Dead of drinking bulls' blood in Persia, Aristotle,
Whose thin smiling lips pass softly
In the color of my mind.

Fierce blood informing the veins
Beats on a measured drum; my tolling heart
Beats the bronze bell of Rome; the legion in unison
Bronze; and the trumpet throat of Antony[21]
Ringing bronze, and the screaming eagle

18. After Zeus, Phoebus Apollo was the most revered of the Greek gods, often pictured with a bow and a lyre; the former signified distance from the gods, as well as death, terror, and awe, while the latter proclaimed communion with the gods via music, poetry, and dance. Phoebus means bright, and so he was also connected with the sun.

19. Greek god of shepherds and flocks, hunting, rustic music, and nature.

20. Themistocles (524-460 BC) was the Athenian politician and naval strategist who created Athens' powerful navy. He is credited with saving Greece from subjection to the Persian Empire at the battle of Salamis in 480 BC.

21. Marcus Antonius (83-30 BC), more commonly known as Mark Antony, was a Roman general and politician who served faithfully under Julius Caesar.

Stern as a sword; and the bronze amphitheater bearing dark arches
Groined with lean ribs of metal. Issuing, the lion
Brings clangor and killing over the arena
Lifting a brazen heaven; the scornful neck of a god
Bending transcendent eyes, embodied
Corinthian bronze, bright as a wolf.

The Rome is calamitous metal,
Smelted with kingly sweat, refined in annihilation,
Cast in a flowing fire like the strange bronze
Out of the temple treasury; integral,
This Rome, of secret Etruria[22] and the clear mind alloyed
Into the strict admirable shape of a trumpet.

I have listened to the bright pattern of a trumpet
Crying against barbarians, I have seen
Horses reared over my body pawing at air
In the crazy silence of lightning; I in my body
Have taken the fierce weight of a man on the Roman sword.
And I have felt the javelin dividing my body
Sharp as sea water; no dream, but a fire
In the remembering blood, while seven hills
Live in the wavering air, who possess my spirit
With thunderous profiles, like secular echoes of the Caesars
Carved imperially in resounding brass.

The crested eagles are broken; Rome is fallen.
The temple roof has fallen in. Survival
Comes like a miser to the dead.
These had cruel hands, the strong bone jointed to bone,
Sinew and nerve shaped to a weapon; narrow bodies
And twisting lips, and nostrils sucking air,
And secret eyelids; now in immortal marble
The immense and silent thunder of that blind stare
Fronts life; and these were the semblance of male swords

22. Ancient central Italy.

Now broken; these with the sharp flesh of emperors
Impaled desirous nations; insecurely
Their blunted fingers fumble at my thought
Softly as a nuzzling child.

With the passion of dead faces
They crave a thin vitality; Tiberius,[23] hot and ruinous,
The acrid mouth of Nero;[24] curling warm laughter
In the mouth of Lucius Verus;[25] Hadrian's[26] lover,
A face of honey, bitterly haunted.
The peering thin mask of a boy
Pursues, made of delicate bones and lips; Caligula,[27]
The inconsiderable fragment of divinity.

The voices fall away like dreams; they wander
Imponderably as dreaming. They are withered
Like dead grass trivially; and the great brazen throat of alarums
Whispers only a sound of rasping silver
Like wind against metal. Long after,
In signs and wonders, the Emperor Julian[28] despairing
Comes to make figs of thistles, gold of wheatstraw
And gods of rotten dust.

Bitter philosopher,
Broken upon the fangs of unmerciful beauty,

23. Born Tiberius Claudius Nero (42 BC–AD 37), he reigned as Roman emperor AD 14 to 37.

24. Born Nero Claudius Caesar Augustus Germanicus (37-68), he was Roman emperor from 54 to 68.

25. Born Lucius Aurelius Verus Augustus (130-169), he was Roman emperor from 161 to 169.

26. Born Publius Aelius Hadrianus Augustus (76-138), he was Roman emperor from 117 to 138.

27. Caligula, born Gaius Caesar Germanicus (12-41), was Roman emperor from 37 to 41.

28. Julian, born Flavius Claudius Julianus Augustus (331 or 332–363), was Roman emperor from 361 to 363. He was also known as Julian the Apostate and Julian the Philosopher.

Tattered by loving, shaken like a rat by strength,
A leopard of defiance, spotted fire
Leaping at spears; a shrill steel-colored eagle
Screaming the human brain against the unanswering sky,
And trapped, snared, shattered like leaves, destroyed, dishonored,
Cast among unavailing gods and abortive temples
In the blank desert, to die of a fever
And the fever of his thought, and the world
Lost in a desert.
This was the gallant flesh and excellent pain of humanity,
Julian, who loved the dead.

They are betrayed,
Tricked softly by desire, led along easy ways
And delicate alcoves, fattened upon splendors,
Enriched to the fine artifice of many perfections
For an outrageous rapine. Arising
A bubble of spirit blown from dying lips
Stares with lost eyes at defeat. Frustration
Compels the inveterate custom of universes
To burst in wandering fire.

Violated by daggers,
Disdained, flung askew on the chequered tiles of the Senate House,
Empty as a sanctuary, striped with purple blood
And broken like tinsel glass, Julius Caesar[29]
Comes upon the hurried salvage of three slaves
Bearing homeward a robe of purple and a lean corpse
With one arm hanging down.

Silent intensities of thought like the track of a meteor
Come to destruction.
The swift fire, the conquering passion, laughter cracking the planet

29. Born Gaius Julius Caesar Octavianus Augustus (100-44 BC), he ruled Rome
from 46 to 44 BC; he was assassinated by members of the Senate, including Gaius
Cassius Longinus and Marcus Junius Brutus.

To its roaring kernel, shaking the long seas, lifting
A superb act and a miraculous intention
Come to destruction.
And the thin curve of eyelids flickering,
Thin shoulder-bones, and the structural skull,
And the unimaginable contrivance of hands
Precious as masculine gems; and a recondite mouth
Unrelenting, unloving, sweeter than fire, and smiling,
Come at last to a sudden flurry of wet blood,
A slack arm swinging, in the dusty air
Lean, corded, swinging down and up and down,
And presently to nothing.

There is no more to say
Unless his forehead caught a journeying star
That rose above the burning. There were tears
And blood, the strange threatening of blood, and a long wail
Of something inexpressibly old and sad,
All night, the moaning Jews. A star grew between
The two cupped hands of Caesar, in whose reflection
He shone a manifest god. There is no more
Than truth, than lie, to hold the ominous wave
Curling above the world. No death
Shall crash upon me, nor the claws of doom
Pluck at my body and rive the shuddering spirit
From its last love, while within the star
Immortal Caesar lives. There is no longer
The barricade for chaos; no fabricated sphere,
A turning planet, thin reality,
This color on the wind,
Ghost, fading ghost;
And desolation.

(March 1936)

Snow in Madrid[30]

Softly, so casual,
Lovely, so light, so light,
The cruel sky lets fall
Something one does not fight.

How tenderly to crown
The brutal year
The clouds send something down
That one need not fear.

Men before perishing
See with unwounded eye
For once a gentle thing
Fall from the sky.

(December 1937)

Cadence on a Stolen Line

Rain rings in water silverly,
rain rings in water;
whether the sky lets down a thread
of spider weaving grey with a little light
from thick clouds spinning water;
whether the river puts upward lilies thinly
and faint tulips, sharp sprays of water,
flowers whose blood in miraculous chilly courses
freezes the air, silverly comes the rain
and silver, and hesitating, lines of ripples
crossed with a shower;
evasive water shines and the shore grows pale,

30. Reprinted in *War Poems of the United Nations*, ed. Joy Davidman (New York: Dial Press, 1943), 301-2.

the blunt clouds luminous; taste now in the air
diffused and smiling rain.

(April 1937)

Night-Piece

I shall make rings around you. Fortresses
In a close architecture of wall upon wall,
Rib, jointed rock, and hard surrounding steel
Compel you into the narrow compass of my blood
Where you may beat forever and be perfect,
Keep warm. The blood will keep you warm, the body
Will curl upon you not to let the air
Sting you with ice. And you shall never be wounded
By your bright hostile business of living, while
I and my charitable flesh survive.

Interminably
I shall come with windings and evasions, I shall bar
My lover from the aggression of a star
Cold, unperturbed, and meaning death. Nor shall you
Suffer one touch of pain or recollection of evil
While you are in my bed; nor shall you suffer
The old iniquities of the universe
If I will have you safe.

Now the first ring
Is the devious course of my blood going all around you
And you with a blind mouth growing in my flesh
In the likeness of a child. You cannot break free,
For I have locked a little of your life
Into my life; and the second ring to enclose you
My breast and arms; then a smooth round of light
And a wall winking with sleek and brittle windows
With darkness cowering at them; the cold starry endless enemy

Crowding you in, crushing my arms around you
To keep off black terrors. For one more magic circle
I have the world.

Now in a ring of ocean
Far away, there is a hollow island holding
A flat blue pool, holding a bird. They kill the bird
To find a round egg covering one round nutshell
That hides the smallest yellow oval grain
Of wheat that ever had a life for kernel;
They shall not find your life. Lie and keep warm
In your own rolling planetary shell; keep warm,
My lover. Lie down lover. If there is peace
Arrested in any memorable fragment of time
I have shut you in with it and drawn circle.

(*January* 1937)

Survey Mankind

If we could set our teeth in the hide of America,
clasp her fat hills to our faces and be nourished by them,
we could not love her better. Along roads
we have gone loving the grassroot in the ditch
and the good smell of grass burning, and the fires.
We have touched this country; we have seen it; we have heard it
        with our ears.
We have known the hooked rugs. We have watched the honey
bright golden standing for sale. Tumbleweed
blows along the American highways like our minds.

And we have counted the places, one by one;
the desert towns, the blown trees edging the prairie
meant to break the wind, and the abandoned filling stations
and the places where jackrabbits jump out of the night.
We have understood all these things and held them in our minds,

and we have counted the people, one by one;
the faces seen under lights; the church sociable; the miners at
    evening
and the boy behind lunch counters in the blue early morning.
And we have spoken to them, one by one.

We have seen America staring in the desert
and the pinched child's face at the cabin door.
Look at this with us;

under sun and rain
ponder upon the mountains and the plain.
Weigh in your hands the gold and the pain.

And in Dakota the houses have turned yellow,
the paint scoured from their sides with dust; the earth
baked and split like a bruised lip; the grass
sends roots five feet down for water; (the roots remain,
only the roots remain).

And elsewhere rain is shaken from the edge of leaves.
Look at this with us.

We have lain awake
all night and listened. We have loved the sound
of the corn grown out of American ground.
We have climbed into our cars and driven out
past many telegraph poles, along the sleek highway
shining so well it looks wet ahead of us.
And we will make America a fine place,
a province for the men in it; we will make
the gold corn and the water to be for all.

Come and see.
Partake of this bread. Come riding. Devour this country
with your eyes and heart, the barren and fertile soil.
Come and see the red earth and the black earth and the desolation.

The grasshopper cries forever. Our ears
are filled with the dry rustling of leaves. All night
the sharp tin sound of grasshoppers possesses us.

Sit down in the desert, take the sagebrush in your hand;
here are big jackrabbits and birds with black and white wings,
and the cactus, and the red rock. Euphorbia[31]
points heavily at the sun. In the desert we suck oranges.

O dear darkness
descend upon us, blacken the sky with night,
remove the sun from our eyes. Darkness
come up in the desert with wind. And we shall
and we shall drink green and yellow pop out of bottles
and in order to buy hamburgers we shall stop at the next roadside
      stand.
They will give us a place to wash, because we wear America in-
      grained in our faces.

And we shall go again. We shall go through the rain,
the silver sweet mist being about us again,
the mountains being about us; the snow
breathing sharply in the air.

And we shall come
to the wide golden western cities of the plain
put between mountains and sea and spiced with
orange trees, the persimmon, the peach, the white and purple figs.
Many pounds of grapes are bought for very little money.
We shall see the Pacific like soft cream upon the pebbles
and scatter with our fingers the wave's edge
warm on the shore. Behind us
lies spread the body of America,
corn in Iowa, rice in the South, and the wheatfields,
the fruit and bread. The precious bread. The bread.

31. Euphorbia, sometimes referred to as spurge, is a large class of flowering plants
normally found in arid regions.

Break a wheatstraw and bring it home.
This is your share of America.
The earth is possessed and used evilly; the many rivers
make paid lightning over wires. The many trees
headless have gone heavily down the river.
Break a stalk of cactus and take it home with you
and do not question why the thorns cause you pain;
this is what you are given out of the plain.
Now with me bow down and love this earth
which you have not had for your own; touch it with your forehead.
Repair its wounds with the piety of your fingers.
You will make it a fine earth belonging to its people.

You are essential here. You are the rock. The Mississippi
flows through your arteries from skull to ankle-bone.
Your tongue is taught by these birds;
                              the grasshopper
ticks in your blood. You are by this begotten
autochthon;[32] earth-engendered; acacia of this soil,
red flowers of this desert.

Now with me
bow and set your mouth against America
which you will make fine and the treasure of its men,
which you will give to the workers and to those who turn land over
        with the plow.

(June 1938)

The Alchemist

In a jealous delight
I adore in the sun
Thin grapes holding light
In a sweet golden skin.

32. An indigenous person or earliest known inhabitant.

A miraculous whirl
Or an ardent vapor,
The gold flames curl
At the tip of a taper.

Gold circles for eyes
Look out of birds;
The sleek beetle flies
Spreading gold shards.

Autumn wears fiery gold,
Orange and sullen,
Velvet as marigold,
Hazy as mullein,

Whose warm flowers mellow
The pungent fern;
Silver and yellow
Their tall fires burn.

Thick honey and amber
Color the air;
Like a tawny brown ember
Pheasant wings flare

With a feathered gold whir
Out of shining rocks
At the fierce-colored fur
And gold eyes of a fox.

— The magnificent smith
Whips his gold sweet and cruel,
To a thorny frame with
His pride for a jewel.

His hands and sorrow
Shape various gold

Chaste as an arrow,
Or florid, enscrolled

For the lusting of kings;
Filed sharp into dragons
With filigree wings;
Or a revel of flagons,

Brown clear like a petal,
Or hammered in bars,
Such sorcerous metal
Lives in the stars.

Green moonlight has gold,
And gold, the sun;
My fire is cold;
I have none.

(December 1935)

Il Pleure dans Mon Coeur[33]

How shall I keep the rain from my eyes;
how shall I walk discreetly in the sky,

33. The title means "It rains in my heart." Davidman borrowed it from Paul Verlaine's poem of the same name:

> Il pleure dans mon Coeur
> Comme il pleut sur la ville.
> Quelle est cette langueur
> Qui pénêtre mon coeur?
>
> O bruit doux de la pluie
> Par terre et sur les toits!
> Pour un coeur qui s'ennuie,
> O le chant de la pluie!
>
> Il pleure sans raison
> Dans ce coeur qui s'écoeure.

keep my feet safe and keep my honor dry,
how shall I flourish comforted and wise:

who will guard me from the slow rain coming down
dappling the air with light;
who will keep the rain from my sight
and who will shut my door that I may not drown

overtaken by the soft flood of the rain
that fingers patiently the eyes and hair,
and when shall I no longer stare
at a starred melancholy windowpane....

Only turn your lips to my lips and let your hair
lie in my hand or tangle in my hand,
and fall asleep, and let your body stand
between my sorrow and the weeping air.

(January 1938)

Lament for Evolution

Apollo, having been given my desire,
my ancient passion, my desire, my lover,
I find my answer is no more than emptiness
and a bitter taste; yet praising Apollo, craving
only the soft and friendly unconsciousness of the beasts
outdistanced, I give thanks; I return thanks for the admirable
    delusion,

Quoi! nulle trahison?
Ce deuil est sans raison.

C'est bien la pire peine
De ne savoir pourquoi,
Sans amour et sans haine,
Mon coeur a tant de peine.

the bright and soundless explosion of my world
which might have meant fires, instead collapsing
flaccid into the shape of bitterness.

Never the intrinsic sun spawned in a body
so tight and perfect a serpent, Apollo;
never your sunlight on your lover's lip
stung with so cruel, so salt and beautiful a virtue;
never before so nakedly pain
struck the eyes sculptural. Bitter crusts of salt
freeze my eyes white and cold. Apollo,
never your sunlight, never your lean marble
stretched shuddering like my body like a wire. Pure, narrow,
the mind extends itself against the winds,
barren as its own smiling tooth.

Bitterness in the tooth
devours and poisons; whose flesh envenomed
yields blood to the cannibal maceration of self
feeding on self. Bitterness on the lips
tastes more profound than kisses. Bitterness
seeps down the throat into hollows, pits of destruction, laboring
        channels
where my fine pain creates itself to remain alive
with a sweet functional music, while bitterness
mews at my ear like a cat.

Bright, acrid blood upon a bitten tongue,
the fine, ultimate, perfect taste of blood
completes desire. I, feeding upon myself,
lecherous in the satisfaction of myself, pure as a circle
in the round whole of myself, taste my blood;
my mouth, thick and strangling, eats divinity
repugnant to the guts;

these guts being sweet and wholesome,
untroubled by realization, smirking profoundly,

discreetly making flesh, and if at times
confused and bubbling with odd stresses of emotion
they belch and sleep again. They are not I
myself, the nodding, grinning, thinking sack, the impossible
laughter of self against self, created in jelly
to hate and make conjectures.

Topped with brain
the whole blind and happy edifice of guts
tumbles into despair. Besieged with sweet sounds,
environed by odors, ambushed by delectations,
the brain grows sweetly drunk on itself; thereafter
sits in sour vomit and chews on bitterness.

It is bitterness to know that I am alive;
it is bitterness to find no reason for life, Apollo,
except the subterfuge and apology of dying,
and to fear death, knowing the flesh will crawl,
nerves, bubbling glands, voracious guts, crawl screaming
away from dying. It is bitterness
in knowing life, anticipating death, playing softly with emotions,
to feel the blind slug brain recoil, turn inward,
and love its own contemplating lunatic eyes
sick with disgust; it is I, Apollo.

(December 1936)

Japanese Print

How the pale quiet gulls whitely arrayed on air
make long lines flying; how sweet the scythe,
the blade, the wing; how clearly come the narrow
beloved quiet curvings into sleep.

Absently twilight
trailing upon the endless, blue, predestinate sky

illumines ripples; how the narrow moon
luminous rides the figured air as silver
as slanted water lightly brushed with wings.

Fairer than any waters,
delectable; O cool, forgetful, how little light flows over
shivering along a million wings and stars.

(March 1937)

This Woman

Now do not put a ribbon in your hair;
Abjure the spangled insult of design,
The filigree sterility, nor twine
A flower with your strength; go bare, go bare.

The elements foregathered at your birth
Gave your hard throat an armor for despair,
Burned you and bathed you, nourished you with air,
And carved your body like a tree of earth.

This is the symbol that I shape of you;
Branching from the broad column of your flesh
Into the obdurate and fibrous mesh
Stubborn to break apart and stiff to hew;
Lost at your core a living skeleton
Like sharp roots pointing downward from the sun.

(June 1934)

For the Revolution

This man, this ape with laughter in his mouth,
this ape with salt crusts stiffening his eyes,
this laugher and weeper, mongrel of grief and laughter,
spoiler of flesh, this breed of devastations,
this froth of blood and bone and passion and dreaming
corrupts on the earth; is rotten.

And when panic takes him
he will blacken the sweetness of the earth. And when hunger takes
     him
he will eat the members of his children.
He is full of shame; he is foul; he squats among the bones.

But he has told me
(this man, this fine miraculous slime, this murder)
he has told me that he will give himself bread;
he has told me that he will make himself a fine house
and there shall be no hatred in it, nor lies.
I have heard his voice. He will have peace and bread.

The man will clean his own blood from his fingers.
He with his own hand will create himself.
He must come gilded with his own redemption.

Who else shall come,
what other shape, what more uplifted spirit,
wing at his shoulder, angel on his lip,
shall come to bury us;
                    and on this ruin
make the new earth out of pure gold and air
and the new city. For who else shall come;
neither the insect nor the son of god,
not the wise carrion-beetle nor the archangel Gabriel
annunciator of the kingdom of heaven,
nor the archangel Michael with the sword.

Nothing will be done that the hands of man cannot do,
nothing will be digged that he cannot dig with his fingernails,
nothing will be made and eaten without his teeth.

But he has said, this man. I have heard him speak.
He will come out of the black hell of the mine.
He will come out of the fire and forging steel,
the hell of the boiler room, the prison hell,
the whirring hell of the factory; and when he comes
we shall not need archangels. We shall need
only the salt and human loins of this man
and the sweat marking with grime the lines of his palm,
and he will make out of the angry storm,
the brutal stone, the sea, the supple water,
the iron mountains and the fertile soil
the everlasting image of this man.

                                        (*March* 1938)

Obsession

I have not forgiven my enemy
The splendor of the eyes in his skull
Or that his mouth is good to see
Or that his thought is beautiful.

I have given my hatred food to eat
Thinking his body so fine a thing
One shall not find the milky wheat
Or the new bread more nourishing,

Or more desirable fine gold,
Or lovelier silver thrice refined;
And I have kept me warm in the cold
Hating the valor of his mind.

This hate is honey to my tongue
And rubies spread before my eye,
Sweet in the ear as any song;
What should I do, if he should die?

(January 1938)

Sorceress Eclogue[34]

(*Ducite ab urbe* ...[35])

Now under rainstorm corn is come again
and it shall ripen into the body of my love.

Now birdseed scattered falling makes again the summer
burning with leaves, bringing the pollen grain,
the rain falling like seed the firseed fallen
the honey thick in trees and the smell of rain
and the bird crying alone. I for my lover
cook magic over woodfires to call him home.

If he will come to me with the smell of
woodsmoke and he will come to me with the burning of
leaves and the slow smoke upward in the night,
he will have his skin dappled with the shadow of leaves
faunskin; he will be spotted like the spotted cat
under the turning of leaves dark and bright.

This is magic made with a leaf and a leaf;
by this incantation his body drawn home.

O by the wings of leaves across the city
call him from the thick city roofs;
call him louder than automobile horns

34. An eclogue is a short, pastoral poem.
35. Latin for "Draw from town."

and he will come with his eyes shut walking lightly
over sharp stubble in grainfields
                                        pricking his feet
on light and glittering dead blades
                                    the sun
friendly on the skin of his arms and the sweat
salt on his lip;
sleepwalker my lover by this incantation
he will come sleeping in the sunlight.
(I shall kiss you with your mouth sticky with honey
your eyelids stuck together with sleep;
                                        the summer
shall enclose us in the heavy heat.)

This incantation is made like a blade of corn
and it will shape his body in the air
like the new kernel of the corn stripped bare;
this magic is the tassel of the corn
dripping pollen through the simmering air;

between the willow and the poplar tree
between the willow tree and the oak sapling
tiger striped with dark or gold of leaves
and the rain lying on leaves like shivering glass
the shape of his voice like the round sunlight dropping;
wearing no clothing upon him but the wheaten sunlight
and the good smell of his body;
                                    the sun
glinting on his fingernails.

I am the earth of which the corn is grown.
This incantation shall raise up the corn
and it shall walk upon the feet of a man
and wear the mortal forehead of my love.

And it shall come upon me with a talking
of the warm grass at the passage of my love.

I shall take the ashes of the sacrifice
and cast them backward into river water
and I shall break his body on the altar
made out of wax;
                    sweeten the fire with spice;
take bread and wine and give them to this flame
and give three hairs of his head to the fingering wind
and this shall bring him when I say his name.

(I shall put my hands over your hands
and feel the blood beginning in your arm
and run my hands over the hair on your arm.)

                                                        (July 1938)

Prayer against Barrenness

O agony, burn at my heart;
Burn at my heart and keep me warm.
Deliver me from the harsh iron of winter,
Unclothe me of the silver fur of frost,
Pare away the ice from the ends of my fingers.
Set me free of cold idleness
And deliver me from the barrier across my tongue
For I will say my word.
This is winter and I am imprisoned in it
With the tips of my fingers slowly turning to ice
But I shall not forget words
And the beautiful ringing of words linked together,
And I shall remember compassion
And keep my heart lit with a fire of pain
And let the sound of suffering made music
Whistle and sing in my throat until I die.

Here is my breath come whistling from the lung
That I may speak of the desire of my hands

For other hands, and here is my forehead
Where I keep thought, and here is the flesh of my heart
Where I have gathered blood and pain.
Here are the beautiful agonies of living
Spread before my eyes by the sun and moon
Or generously fed to my ears by the air.
This is the stuff of words and I shall speak them;
Let pain melt the ice from the root of my tongue
And from the roof of my mouth. Let passion
Come in the shape of a sword against winter and set me free.

I will take the curious joints of my fingers
And the innumerable thoughts of my brain
And I will take my hair and my lips and my desires
And the sunsets that have passed before me
And the many odors which have delighted my nostrils.
I will make a burnt offering of all these things
Of which the fire shall strengthen my heart.
Surely I shall feel words thicken upon my tongue
And surely I shall possess the words that are needful to me.

(January 1938)

Fly in Amber

Black sky seeps through the windowpane
And crowds my thoughts behind my eyes,
And lightly in the locked skull lies
Over the arches of my brain.

This is my little cell of light,
Floating in vague and vacant air;
This trivial roof and wall I wear,
Caparisoned[36] against the night.

36. Trapped.

The floor is friendly brown and warm,
The ceiling sharp and clear and high;
The amiable chairs and I
Are softly hiding from a storm.

Devious lightning at the door
Claws with quicksilver fingertips;
I make thin music with my lips
Against the elemental roar.

While I have light above my head
And silken things upon my skin
The universe will not come in
To whisper answers to my dread,

Or ruin violate the prim
And crystal insecurity
That clocks and china offer me.
The candlelight is growing dim.

(September 1933)

Prothalamion[37]

Who is this who is coming;
not less than the desire of wind
shall the hungry heart desire the sound;
not less than the rain walks
shall he walk upon the barren ground;
who is this who is coming:
the shadow bearing light
the awful spirit bearing brightness
the shadow with the light about his feet;
not less than the sun walks

37. A prothalamion is a song or poem celebrating a marriage.

shall he tread upon the edge of night.
Who is this who is coming
as the blue heron slantwise upon the wind
coasts from edge to edge of the water and reeds
as the feathers spread thin upon the air;
who is this with shining in his hair
who is this come quietly as the dripping mist
comes down upon the midnight and makes no sound;
who is this who is coming:
he is quiet as a river running underground.

Open the door of the room to him that is come,
that he may enter quietly and take possession;
make soft the path upon the floor of the room;
open the arms of the woman to him
that he may take possession;
open the body of the woman
that his seed may be acceptable into her womb.

(July 1938)

Yet One More Spring

What will come of me
After the fern has feathered from my brain
And the rosetree out of my blood; what will come of me
In the end, under the rainy locustblossom
Shaking its honey out on springtime air
Under the wind, under the stooping sky?
What will come of me and shall I lie
Voiceless forever in earth and unremembered,
And be forever the cold green blood of flowers
And speak forever with the tongue of grass
Unsyllabled, and sound no louder
Than the slow falling downward of white water,
And only speak the quickened sandgrain stirring,

Only the whisper of the leaf unfolding,
Only the tongue of leaves forever and ever?

Out of my heart the bloodroot,
Out of my tongue the rose,
Out of my bone the jointed corn,
Out of my fiber trees.
Out of my mouth a sunflower,
And from my fingers vines,
And the rank dandelion shall laugh from my loins
Over million-seeded earth; but out of my heart,
Core of my heart, blood of my heart, the bloodroot
Coming to lift a petal in peril of snow,
Coming to dribble from a broken stem
Bitterly the bright color of blood forever.

But I would be more than a cold voice of flowers
And more than water, more than sprouting earth
Under the quiet passion of the spring;
I would leave you the trouble of my heart
To trouble you at evening; I would perplex you
With lightning coming and going about my head,
Outrageous signs, and wonders; I would leave you
The shape of my body filled with images,
The shape of my mind filled with imaginations,
The shape of myself. I would create myself
In a little fume of words and leave my words
After my death to kiss you forever and ever.

(*January* 1938)

Near Catalonia[38]

We have the sweet noise of the sea at our back
and before us the bitter shouting of the gun;
and the brass wing of aeroplanes and the sun
that walks above us burning. Here we wound
our feet on metal fragments of the bomb,
the sword unburied and the poisoned ground.
Here we stand; here we lie; here we must see
what we can find potent and good to set
between the Fascist and the deep blue sea.

If we had bricks that could make a wall we would use them,
but bricks will break under a cannonball;
if we had iron we would make a wall,
but iron rings and splinters at the bomb,
and wings go across the sky and over a wall,
and if we made a barrier with our earth
they would murder the earth with Fascist poison,
and no one will give us iron for the wall.
We have only the bodies of men to put together,
the wincing flesh, the peeled white forking stick,
easily broken, easily made sick,
frightened of pain and spoiled by evil weather;
we have only the most brittle of all things the man
and the heart the most iron admirable thing of all,
and putting these together we make a wall.

(*March 1938*)

38. First published in *New Masses* 29 (October 18, 1938): 18. Catalonia is an autonomous community in northeastern Spain.

Four Elements

Earth and water, air and fire,
Living in hot wombs conspire
To an end; and snarl and mingle
Yellow clay, with spikes that tingle
Watery, blue, an evanescent
Flash of frosty and lactescent[39]
Ice; red iron in a pool,
Cold fireflies, fishes, and the cool
Immeasurable air of breath,
And the strict bones of narrow death;
Lights and lashes in the seas
By the fluke of a forked whale; these
In a place dissolve and seethe,
Shape my name and let it breathe,
The worms feed and stars aspire;
Air, the waters, earth and fire.

Of such flame together met
Is my body's metal set;
Through me gnome and undine[40] wander,
Elf and sylph[41] and salamander
Ride the courses of my blood,
That it ripen red and good;
Gross and subtle element,
Brown or fiery, they are blent
In a carnal alkahest;[42]
Knotted in the fiber nest
Of serpent nerve, the devious
Impulse strikes and sings at us.
Gnomes in caverns of a lust
Lie prurient in itching dust

39. Milky.
40. A water nymph.
41. An imaginary spirit of the air.
42. A hypothetical universal solvent sought by alchemists.

Till alarums dark or clear
Whirling round a spiral ear
Tick in byways of ourselves
Whispers of the running elves;
Till the architectural
Flesh is blown ephemeral,
Thin as dust and heavy haze,
Or a tissue like a maze,
Where writhing, writhing, out or in
Physical serpents will begin,
Littered by the dragon-snake
Where the earth lips over black,
Hollow out of light; therefrom
Issue serpent and the gnome,
Who threading in a bloody mesh
Play destruction with the flesh.

Craving burns this jointed earth
Like a male and dragon birth;
Animals of iron and stone
Savagely creak and trample upon
These raggedly quicksilver nerves;
This is the end the earthworm serves.

Undines arching like a wind
Fill the circles of my mind
Where the troubling waters hiss
And surge creative; what is this
Echo of myself I see
Swimming drowned in silver sea
Where the ripple moves in rings
And a smothered ocean sings?
Sea-fans painted full of eyes
Watch the fractured waters rise
Crossed with bubbles; at my throat
Musically springs a note;
Hear the water singing thin

Like a watery violin
Flow behind my eyes and make
Flowing light in arrows wake;
Green under corners of the world
Undulate and whiten; curled
Bubbles slightly flower up
In the two hands' sacred cup.
Answers to the water tones
Blow in ribbons through my bones.

Who is this within the sea?
I and undine liquidly
Singing, find a silver one
Changing what my throat has done
Into sound that waters know,
And singing. To this end they flow
Upon me, who surrendering
Hear the undines float and sing.

Sylphs descend a snarling air
Shaggy with the bitter hair
Of storm, blown thin and spidery tangling
Cloud; they bellow with a jangling
Thunder striking sharp and loud
From the savagery of cloud.
Fiery rectilinear
Lightning licks the prickled air,
Whose abrupt and crystalline fires
Crowd my thought with shining wires,
Terse and mental arabesques,
Triangles and twirling disks
That of moving linear wind
Shape fine alchemies of the mind,
Whose slender edifices are
Clearer than a frozen star
Where the soft imponderable ghost
Of plashing air is flared and lost;

Whose echoes, like the glimmering stone
Of a grey and solid sun
Hanging in his liquid sky
Thick and bright as mercury,
Wake the smooth and luminous
Quietude in shivering space.

Here the sylphs unfurl alone,
Each an artifice of bone
Spread against an airless light,
Musical and strict and white;
Tricks of interweaving line
In a cold and silver design
Build within my narrow skull
The geometric miracle
Of thought; and servant to an end
Winds and the rapid sylphs descend.

Salamanders in their fire
Live remembering desire
And pain, and wait to wake anew
The arrow pain that flashes through
Fiery nerves, at thought of whom
Years have nibbled in a tomb;
All the subtle lustrous kings
Strong as dragons, flowerings
Of spider passions, bearing wise
Hands and lips and curving eyes.
What they wanted, what they were
Weigh lighter than the bitter air.
The lovely turning of a head
Goes; and many words have said
This, that valor perishes.

The salamander cherishes
The bodily precise attire
Of living, with intrinsic fire

Cruel at the core, and orange heat
Dancing in the bloody beat;
Poor bodies for a precious fuel
Nourish grief, wherein the jewel
Beast of centered fire resides,
Eyed like honey. And it glides
With the fiery feet and hands
Through these locked and fleshly strands,
Burning, simmering in tears,
And burning. Miseries and fears,
Crawling loves for this are met,
Velleities,[43] perhaps regret;
Here the yellow lizard sends
A sting to answer fiery ends.

Out of tangled element
Only mystery is blent;
Water, earth, and fire and air
Send their servant minister
To conjure fractions of the whole
In one multicolored soul.

(April 1936)

The Empress Changes Lovers

You'd let me fall in a bundle of wet rags
Put off; you'd peel me off like serpent clothing
Flaked, sloughed, discarded, frittered off, but you find
Discarding me, I should be there to plague you
With my faint eyes too easily remembered
Staining your mind like smoke. Thereupon you find
You'll not have me, nor your desire, nor my arrogance
Printed upon your world; nor the smallest part of my flesh

---

43. Wishes, desires, or inclinations without accompanying actions.

That might serve to speak to you, and for such a riddance
Murder being quietly inadequate, you'll command
And I am dead with surprising public splendors;
That thereby all the abolition you can publish
Of my body, my touch on your arms, my love in your love
And your weak yielding secretly encountered
May trumpet me formally and imperially null.

For you must kill what you can. Let no recollection
Of any time when you were a woman come
Grinning at you with mortality written on bare teeth;
And I made tatters would not survive to alarm you
By so much as the last bone of a finger
Unconsumed that knows your breast. To this end light fires.
Only it will not serve; you shall recall
Forever the tingle and flash of my body embracing you,
The way my strength came forth, the angles of my elbows,
The placing of my ribs, long clasps of thighs
And a flat back; you'll not obliterate
Any of my tricks of touching you to give you pleasure,
And worse for you you'll not forget your pleasure,
As thus and thus you prickled up your skin
And licked out with your rough dry catlike tongue
To which I tasted salt. Kill what you like;
You will not kill the antic of your own body
That remembers me, nor the words, the physical attitudes
And warm rooms, qualities of light, and secretive fabrics
That mean my name; the very smell of my flesh in passion.
But you'll remember, and you will regret
As long as flesh likes pleasant things, and the tenderness
By me created in you will absently come to haunt you
Without a name, and faceless, dumb, and eyeless
Ask for my body.

Will you know where to find my body
Then, will you hold me present to your senses
And hard, and loving, and anything but ashes?

Whatever anodyne you may discover
Will wear another face and personal hands of its own,
Bring you a different touch and new recollections;
Never your special lust for me and its answer,
And the peculiar and lovely delight you had in me; never
The pleasure your senses got from me merely by wanting.
I'm saying you will not have me ever again;
And that your sudden and imperial flesh
Will doubtless find something irrevocable in destruction.

(*March* 1937)

In Praise of Fascists

What flowers come again
In the track of guns
Spring out of buried men
Whose lost blood runs

Thick and bitter in the root,
Sweet and thin in the stem;
The flowers underfoot
Give thanks to them

Whose numerous gift of death
Feeds liberally
Sweet purple to the heath
And honey to the bee.

And murder's hyacinths
Weave him a crown
By whose beneficence
The bombs come down.

(*November* 1937)

The Lately Dead

We now in the slanting and sober light of autumn
go out of our bodies. Above us
dwindles the sky. The cloud, the wind
fade, and the eyelid falls; farewell above us
the end of autumn leaves, the sun, the silence,
the troubled swallows in the wheeling air.

Mourn for us, swallow, whether tending
northward spring make the trees misty
or autumn steal again the birds from the sky; O swallow
O dip and flash of wings, O swooping sky
feathered and arrowed, swallow mourn for us
left dry upon the earth; over these bones
pour silver of the moon and of the rain,
clothe them with leaves apparel them with winter
make a new flesh of the snow. Yet not this death
O swallow, traveling bird, shall lie forgotten
here in the narrow valley in the furrow
under the turn of the season. Some to the east
fly with the sound of our name over blue seas; some northward
cry us against the fog and some go seaward
giving our voice to the voice of the seagulls of the Atlantic;
we here slain and splintered cry from the bones of Spain
thinner than the sound of birds and fainter
than the snow alighting and farther
than the last doubtful stars, and unforgotten,
unforgotten, unanswered, glorious, unconquerable.

(November 1937)

Little Verse

Do not speak of him
Lest I leave you
To flow like water
About his doorstep

Or like a moth
Touch his eyelids
With sleepy dust;
Or like a lover

Trouble his hearing
With sweet lust;
Or leave my body
Upon his doorstep.

(February 1938)

Division

Behold how sweetly we have come together;
Rich night and air, the dark embracing air
And union of the ceiling and the floor
Enclosing passion; love, cool formal sheets,
And secret wool of blankets. And so sweetly
We come together; so the clasp, the spasm
Answer each other, suitably invent
Exhaustion sweeter than content.

Is there no more
To say? the body answering a body
In its own fashion perfect as a flower;
Is there no more to say? Forget that I love you,
Call me a stranger made of mud and water
Wrapped around thought; elaborated, contorted

145

Mud putting forth its horns in guts and organs
And airy nerves; forget me then, think only
Of a fine complicated human creature
Oddly encountered; is your need of it
The mud incarnate? shall I have of you
The lovely mud, unreasoning, the flesh
Beautifully and unimportantly nourished,
While the irrelevant brain stares off into space
At a blank wall; is there no more to say?
I will not eat you; I desire of you
Not to devour your separate nature; never
Shall I suck out your soul. Let us keep lonely;
But I would see the eyes of loneliness
In your eyes meeting me; I would perceive
In this queer universe, life and the spirit,
And from the locked and isolated self
Salute the world outside.

I clamorous, I the imperative,
I the fond conqueror of your love, the lover,
The lion crying in the wilderness,
I conscious of your life, your thought, your soul
(Call it) now hold your body quite as closely
As one can meet another, and the body
Asks and is satisfied, complete, made perfect,
While the brain stares at nothing.

You are not real.
You are like wood and rock, like earth, like satin;
You are a touch, a taste. You are the animal
Gold rippling thighs of horses; or disturbing
And twisting cats; you are the muscles of tigers,
The objective eyes of owls. You are not life;
I am life. I find your accidental body,
I take you for my pleasure, and all's done;
And I am sweetly fed. No more, no more?

(*February* 1937)

Totentanz[44]

Play sweetly a pavane[45] for the sheeted dead
that on peacock feet they tread again the alleys of the world;
here in the low hour the dead are risen
like smoke like the moon's rags they are uncurled
out of the narrow cellar of their prison;
pipe them up upon the pipes of storm;
let music be whispered strict and discreet;
to silver of the geometric form
their small feet rattle like a castanet.
How beautiful the arches of their feet
articulate the measured minuet.
Click and click upon the flagstones as they pass
their bones beat rhythm slick as bottle glass.

Play tap-dancing for the anklebones of the dead,
shake them out over the seeded world,
let these bones arise and sing;
with what a stripped and expurgated tread
they dance the trees to skeletons of spring;

he slain in the bitter moment between cannon and gun,
he divested of his breath in the lap of desire,
the man eaten blood and body by the sun
and the body fed living to traveling fire;

murdered at birth; in the fine laurel murdered;
the leper and the beaten and the proud,
bastard and pope the fatherless and fathered
wearing this choice democracy the shroud.

Bray now upon the trombone and the horn,
let them jiggle and recoil and leap;

44. The title alludes to the "Dance of the Dead" (1849), a symphonic piece for solo
piano and orchestra by Franz Liszt, who based it on the Gregorian melody *Dies Irae*.
   45. A slow, processional dance.

cockcrow incestuous on the barren morn
begets for these beloved children sleep.

(July 1938)

Againrising

The stroke of six
my soul betrayed;
as the clock ticks
I am unmade;

the clock struck nine;
my life ran down
on gears of time
with a sickened sound.

The noonday struck
a note of pride;
spread on the clock
I was crucified.

The clock struck one,
whose spear, whose dart
transfixed my bone
and narrow heart.

The sound of seven
filled me with bells;
I left great heaven
for little hells;

the midnight let
my blood run out
fierce and red
from my opened mouth.

Great chaos came
to murder me
when the clock named
the hour of three.

The dawn grew wide;
the clock struck five,
and all inside
I was alive.

(July 1938)

Jewess to Aryan

Our veins possess variations; our blood
marches to differing tunes. We were conceived
out of varying earth, and each nourished by sweeter waters
than the composite sea. And you descend
the northern streams; nor what swift waters
and yellow populous foam of rivers unroll in Asia
have borne your body. This is not my root
who evolve viciously in the east,
and am hotly bred; not by the unregenerate waste
of savage rivers. Harsh and fecund water
grows out of my heart. The restless Nile
shaped in minute lizard scales, each curve
and wrinkled face of water, this poisonous Nile
was said to engender serpents. You might distrust me,
might be afraid; you clinging fog, you coward
to eat the body out and leave
my sound flesh corroded. Bloodless, too empty
to occupy me, too evasive
to fill my hands; what are you
that you mean more to the blood within my hands
than their own bubbling blood; that you take the place
in my brain, of my brain? What are you

to involve desire; so breakable, pointless,
no more meaningful than difficult laughter.
I have resented you; a parasite worm
drinking the female. I have needed you
because you were clever, or I liked your hair,
and you were kind. How shall I murder you
for your kindness? I am not capable
for your exquisite indirections; your tenderness
I find too thin. You needed me
to divert your mind, to divert
the thin self-consciousness seeping in your body
into a fictive intensity. You have burned into color
the tissue in me, and burned your fingers
at the surprising conflagration. This is so easily said,
that I love you; but I will not love you
when there is nothing left of me; a gutted carcass
for wind to whistle in; the shell of humanity
outlined in ashes. When I have no more strength
you might be afraid of me.

(May 1936)

To a Fish

When I was seven years old I had
A dream, a dream! I wandered in the sun,
And everywhere the yellow earth was hard
And the grass bent down.
Sun was dry and yellow in the grass-blade
And the skin of earth glistened with sun.

Having put my hand upon the earth
I felt sun filling the palm of my hand;
Having kissed the dust with my mouth
I lay and let the kissing sun be kind;
Having eaten yellow light and warmth
I made the sun my everlasting friend.

Here in my temples and my wrists I wear
Veins of sunlight underneath the skin;
And I keep surly sunlight in my hair
And the sun sits where my thoughts begin;
Forgive me then the fire you cannot bear;
How should I help it, being made of sun?

(*January* 1938)

Waltzing Mouse

Impaled I was when I was born,
caught upon time's nether horn,
murdered through and through with birth,
cankered with corrupted earth,
knives set round about my feet,
wormwood given me to eat.
Every hour of sunlight I
watch my body partly die;
every time the moon goes over
cuts my body from its lover.
Mind they gave me that I make
bitter as a broken snake;
heart they gave me to contrive
I should bleed for all alive,
knowing each man's private pain
as a worm within my brain,
lying nightly down alone
to break my kissing lips on stone.
Slick between my fingers run
sands of time from sun to sun,
grains of hunger and delight,
diapered with dark and bright;
kisses and confusions pass
dribbling through the fat hourglass.
I could never put my arm

round my love to keep him warm
but my clasp must be unloosed
and my love by time seduced.
I shall never keep my grief
longer than a maple leaf
flies between the air and ground;
time shall make my spirit sound
and steal from me before I die
the agony I know is I.
Never joy and never sorrow
but they shall be soiled tomorrow,
but they shall be wine and wheaten
bread that time has drunk and eaten.
Starry pleasures I would cherish
inchmeal dwindle, dim, and perish;
hatred that would keep me clever
shrivels, like a salty river
slaughtered by corroding sand;
treasures cupped within my hand
time has nibbled from my palm;
all my storms decline to calm
dead and level in a breast
time has gelded of unrest,
and I skip from minute to minute
each one with me buried in it,
and I see my bridges burn
gold behind me as I turn,
and I see my painful track
blotted out behind my back
till I die as I was born,
slain upon time's other horn.

(June 1938)

Tortoise

I wear a shell upon myself
To keep myself from coming through;
To make a small and final gulf
Between my living face and you.

And you have had me as you would,
For taste and touch; you have not known
My spirit in the secret blood
Running a trickle through a bone.

Tangible fingers of you find
Sufficient answer, while I take
Evasive refuge in the mind
Or sanctuary in mistake.

I slip the net of you for me
With salvage separate and whole;
A spindrift of an entity
And one cold fraction of my soul,

As fabric out of wind and light
You do not want or would despise,
Ecstatic, innocent, and slight;
And am enabled to devise

Of such imponderable stuff
Armor enclosing silver space
Where I withdraw into the tough
Frustration of a carapace.[46]

(*December* 1934)

46. The hard outer shell of a turtle.

And Pilate Said (for Basil Rathbone)[47]

Pontius Pilate, remembered as a Roman
leaving the shape of a cold hawk on the mind,
is perished. There is no more to find
now than greyness, in starlight
the webby feathers of hawks on chilly wind,
cold crying out of a bird's throat, thin as air, and no man
but is supplanted by nebulous angels. Nor sunlight
cutting and white comes sharp against the dead,
but the throat perishes and the tongue is broken
beyond a whisper forever; nor overtaken
by the slight winds of anything said
in voices, remainders of ashes are shaken
along a thin watery running twilight.

Once in a doubtful year between age and youth
the hawk cried questions in barbarian
lands of confusion, and his answers ran
thick painted noise out of a barbarous mouth,
whereat the hawk disdaining: What is truth?
clamored like starfire from the leaning sky
all shrill with only one sweet murderous cry
tearing fine air;
cry like a talon, like a question, tear
the lying heart, tear loving, tear the heart,
let bravery out, let the clear spirit go fly,
tear nestling bones from anchorage, tear apart
the tender lips, the soft flesh of a lie.

(April 1937)

47. The actor Basil Rathbone portrayed Pilate in the 1935 film *The Last Days of Pompeii*.

Apology for Liberals[48]

Whether the greater or the little death
be more to fear; whether the ominous voice
and iron murder of bombs, the broken forehead,
the limbs left bloody in broken stone, the murder,
the sudden bursting of the flesh asunder
in a red scream, whether the last destruction
be the last degradation; or whether the spirit
stiff and encrusted with lying, the flinching eyes
poor shifts of daily death, the pride
resolved in filth, be a worse worm to bear
than any gnawing the eyeholes of a skull
lost on the battlefield; pity the little death,
fighters pity cowards.

The fear prevails the shame prevails the terror
weakens the cords of the knees and loosens the tongue
and we are wounded by any whisper of music
and we endure barely the weight of a word
and we turn aside. O then be merciful
to the soft hands the delicate torn fingernails
unarmored eyes. Forgive these cowards
for the weak dream; forgive them tremulous,
forgive them broken. Let them come upon
some easy corner of death. Pity these cowards,
you struck into fragments by the bombs, you perishing
under a scream of air and falling steel,
you fighters you fallen in battle.

(*November* 1937)

48. First published in *New Masses* 28 (August 16, 1938): 4.

End of a Revolutionary

When I am born again
I shall come like the grass-blade;
I shall be fertile and small
As the seed of grasses.
Rain shall breed me;
Earth shall bear me;
I shall smell of the sun
Over green fields.

Eyeless under earth
Worms gnaw the rootstock;
The strength of birdwing
Grows out of my seed;
Out of leaf and my stem
I nourish warm cattle,
And I scatter pollen
For the bees to make bread.

When I am come again
I shall be clean
Of the taint of sorrow;
I shall grow lightly
Without any pain;
All that was weariness
Is less than the shadow
When the clouds pass.

I shall come whispering
Together, and breathing
Together, and wordless
Speaking of peace,
And die in winter
And rise in summer
And conquer the earth
In the shape of grass.

(January 1938)

An Absolution

Let the red image of my agony
Move you no more than to a cool regret
For inconsiderable sorrow. Let
The troubled fires of my body be

A thin light in an interstellar cave
Beyond the savage suns; permit your ear
In the harsh wailing of my soul to hear
The shallow music of a little wave.

I will not have you tainted by my pain;
I am scarred and sculptured to a hollow mask
Of vivid torture, yet I am not slain
By sharp contrivances of your disdain;
And for your gentle silence I shall ask
My bitter lunar love to leave you sane.

(August 1933)

Dirge for the Living

Out of our cave;
the earth a wall, the sky a wall, the ocean
a subtle prison and the nostril cave
whereby the life fights outward is a betrayal
letting life in again. Perceive
how we are compassed on all sides; in agony
when sucking at freedom, at burning emptiness
out of space past all time and beyond the world
we breathe in air. Cease air. Deliver us
out of the hand of pain. Deliver us
out of the metal, out of the jaws of rock,
the tangled insult of earth. Set us free
when distant towers are a wound and the sky clamps down

157

over grey naked and quivering spirit in the brain;
the sky is too great a burden, the lips of water
touching our lips devour. Set us free
from eyes letting worlds in and the ears perceiving
the brutal rape of sound; deliver us
from touch and taste; too near
the clamp of matter rounds us in the skull.

Sever the bone annihilate the sinew
stop up the nostril choke the mouth and let us
drift out of matter on wings, and let this bird,
this breath, this little air, go loose upon air,
an eddy of wind, a swirl among the stars;
and let us come to nothing. (November 1937)

Skeleton

Beauty came to me in the shape of a wolf
And stared at me with yellow eyes of a wolf
Desiring the good red heart to gnaw upon,
Coveting the heartstrings;

Beauty came to me in the likeness of a wolf
Saying: I will be fed with the bones of your hands
And the cords of your throat that ripple up and down
Playing at music;

Saying: I will devour the knowledge in your eyes
And the love on your lips shall fill my belly; saying:
Give me your heart and body to feed upon
For I am lean;

Now the light wind lives whistling in my shell
In the heart's place and singing in the skull;
Beauty the wolf has eaten out my soul
And left me empty. (January 1938)

Poems 1939-1940

Brazen Head[1]

At the first ringing of the thunder, saying
Time is: out of the brazen image of all time,
the yellow light spilled on the tops of hills
and the wind beat against the wooden walls,
and the first ringing of the thunder
struck like music in the empty room
and Friar Bacon slept.

The brazen head
speaking in the tongue of revolution
clashed about him in the air like swords.
The clock ticked. The night cried. The words
broke and fell beside the heavy bed
vainly; the friar slept.
                     The waking hour
ticked to destruction.

In that emptiness,
in that breathlessness, in that desolation,

1. This poem appears to be inspired by a quote from *The Honourable History of Friar Bacon and Friar Bungay*, an Elizabethan-era stage comedy by Robert Greene (1558-1592). In scene 9 of the play a brazen head — an artificial head made of brass and under demonic control — speaks three times, saying, "Time Is," "Time Was," and "Time Past."

the moment fixed between the thunder and thunder,
the glaze of ice with the pit of water under,
that heavy hush, that innocence of sound;
the rattling of the rain upon the ground
beat upon the hidden drum of the ear
of the wise man as he slept in bed.

At the second ringing of the thunder, saying
Time was: out of the mouth of brass,
the great rain came out of the broken cloud
striking like driven steel and harsh and loud;
repetition on the beaten grass
like the beating of the drum of the heart
in Friar Bacon's ear. He kept his head
comforted against the linen sheet;
heard nothing but the thudding of his blood
out of the heart sent to the head and feet.

At the third ringing of the thunder, saying
Time is past: the brazen head crashed down;
Friar Bacon woke. Spilt on the floor
the pieces of the inevitable hour
winked and caught the light. Still quivering,
still enchanted, still alive, still bird,
he saw the body of the eternal word
stiffen before his eyes.

O magical friar,
slipping the priestly moment, shivering
on the chill backward of a stale desire;
I too the tiger stumble in my spring.

(January 1939)

The Devil Will Come[2]

Being no less than twenty millions rich,
Faustus[3] will give himself to reverent air,
Riding out to open the World's Fair;[4]
Let not this gold be stifled in a ditch,
Diverted by a skid to either side;
The highway shall be honest, shall be wide,
And lest his shaken sweetbreads should be sore,
The world must sleek the roadway to his door.

Many men will fall behind this year,
Abandoned as time walks; variety of bones
Under the cars, under the cobblestones
Serve for the body of this thoroughfare;
This year men and women will fall behind,
Their lungs exploded and their eyes made blind,
Their mouths frozen, silence on their breath;
This is a year appointed for much death.

Bury them deep under the traveling wheel;
Place the laughing man and the lover
In a good road for the world to travel over;
Bury them beneath the automobile,
Whose melted flesh and bone together make
This paved street for the parade to take,
This bone, this blood; but Faustus' magic wit
Shall build the future factory of it.

Built on the basis of these buried men
We celebrate the wheelbase of the car,
Pointed futureward with headlight-star;

2. First published in *New Masses* 32 (June 27, 1939): 6.
3. This alludes to Christopher Marlowe's *The Tragical History of the Life and Death of Doctor Faustus* (1604), a retelling of the Faust legend — the story of a man who sells his soul to the devil in exchange for worldly pleasures.
4. The World's Fair opened on April 30, 1939, in New York City.

Because they lapse and do not rise again
The brassy bank makes mortgage with their bones
In solemn concord of the building-loans;
The stars move still, time runs, the clock will strike
And Faustus makes his speech before the mike.

The World's Fair opens and the golden key
Unlocks the gates of heaven for the crowd;
The rickshaws run, the subway trains are loud,
And Faustus flowers in photography;
Between the air and the electric light
See Faustus painted on the astonished sight;
Between the neon lights of joy and sorrow
Now showing: Faustus in the World Tomorrow.

He sets his feet upon the iron towers,
A palace and a pylon on each hand;
His shadow purples the imported sand,
The murmurs of his mouth are hothouse flowers.
Replete in fattened leather and in chrome,
His car at evening ferries Faustus home
Musing the gate-receipts, the dancer's knees —
And yet, at midnight, Mephistopheles.[5]

(February 1939)

Cold Water

The fountain shivers in the snow,
whose lines of water
stretch upward bright and blue,
frill and falter,

spilling the sun outward
off the sleek spike

5. Marlowe's devil-figure.

of a straight water-cord
drawn tight,

frayed into sunny silk;
the fountain shivers
in snow colored milkily,
silvered by winter's

icicle fingertip;
sheeted trees
watch the hollow sun drop
and the fountain freeze.   (February 1939)

Villanelle of Bill Benét[6]

I will not hang myself today;
Instead I'll wear my velvet dress
And go to lunch with Bill Benét.

I will have truffles and filet
Mignon topped off with watercress;
I will not hang myself today,

But rack my brain for things to say
Best calculated to impress;
I'll go to lunch with Bill Benét

And try to lead the man astray
With wine and other wickedness;
I will not hang myself today,

6. William Rose Benét (1886-1950), along with several others, established the *Saturday Review of Literature* in 1924. He was a prolific writer, and his book of autobiographical verse, *The Dust Which Is God* (1941), won a Pulitzer Prize for poetry in 1942. He and his brother, Stephen Vincent Benét (1898-1943), were early supporters of Davidman's poetry. For more on Davidman and William Benét, see *Out of My Bone: The Letters of Joy Davidman* (Grand Rapids: Eerdmans, 2009), 16, 33, 79, 81, 99, 103, 107-9 (hereafter *Bone*).

For if he's made of mortal clay
He'll probably — Do I digress?
I'll go to lunch with Bill Benét —

I wish the guy would look my way
And venture just one mild caress!
I will not hang myself today
Till after lunch with Bill Benét!

(February 1939)

Apropos

How do you like her now your love one time
Who died between your hands as softly as a bird
And was buried; hard to find
Now under the close clothing of the grass
Striped with the change of seasons; hardly
Unlike a little earth. Being no more
Than a diversion in Venetian glass,
Not wind or water, she will not survive
In any image of her flesh alive.

But if she whispers nightly at your door
You were well advised to let her in
Whose mark is burned into your marrow-bone;
And though her body be as fine and thin
As thought refined to smaller than a hair,
You will discover it to be your own.

(March 1939)

New Spiritual[7]

Shout like bells across the nation,
Shake your hips and go to town,
Swing a song of revolution,
Do the shag in the name of John Brown.[8]
Hear the jazzband how it sings
John Brown's body muted on the strings.

Whisper revolution on the drum;
John Brown marching with an army of banners
Shaking red on the stormy air;
Whip the music up on the xylophone,
The bass drum, the kettle drum, the snare.

Take the mutes off the strings,
Let freedom ring;
John Brown's body in the Negro throat,
The deep throat of innocence, the throat of virgin gold.
Listen to John Brown shouting in the cold,
Shouting in the night with the trumpet note,
Marching with an army in the narrow street
With the drum, with the horn, with a million pairs of feet.

Take the hands away from the muted throat,
Let it open and sing in the name of John Brown,
Making music shine around the town,
Ringing freedom all around the town.   (April 1939)

7. First published in *Fantasy: A Literary Quarterly with an Emphasis on Poetry* 7, no. 1 (1941): 21-22. This poem, along with "High Yellow" and "So We Can Forget Our Troubles," appeared collectively under the title "Amateur Night in Harlem." "New Spiritual" was reprinted on its own in *Seven Poets in Search of an Answer*, ed. Thomas Yoseloff (New York: Bernard Ackerman, 1944), 36-37.

8. John Brown (1800-1859) was an ardent foe of American slavery and devised a scheme to arm slaves and lead them in a revolt against their masters. On October 16, 1859, he led twenty-one men on a raid of the federal arsenal at Harpers Ferry, Virginia. The revolt was quickly put down, with most of Brown's followers killed or captured. Brown was convicted of treason and hanged on December 2, 1859.

So We Can Forget Our Troubles[9]

Isolated by the shaft of spotlight
In which you put your hands and cigarette smoke,
The dancer fixed and grinning on the stage
Holds a long pirouette from age to age,
Empty for your love and for your look.

The trails of smoke and dust along the light
Shining upon the satin and the face,
Her teeth and the winking of her dress,
Cloak her nebulous before the eye
Under the red moon in the backdrop sky,

This backdrop being the place we all would go,
Set about with trees and curtained with distance,
The fabulous flowers, the legendary snow.
We will escape now on the traveling light,
Back of the voice the silver and the dance,

By doorway of the voice into the palace
Where the backdrop builds beneath the sky
Other twilight and other paradise
In which we leave our eyes and go to sleep
Deep out of trouble, deep in limbo, deep.

(April 1939)

Ten Dead Workers[10]

Over this blood
Stretch the blank shroud,

---

9. First published in *Fantasy: A Literary Quarterly with an Emphasis on Poetry* 7, no. 1 (1941): 22. This poem, along with "High Yellow" and "New Spiritual," appeared collectively under the title "Amateur Night in Harlem."

10. This poem was included in a letter Davidman wrote on April 28, 1939; it was first published in *Bone*, 23.

Modestly cover it;
Lest it offend
Comfortable men,
Put flowers over it;
Use for its sheath
The funeral wreath.

Lest your blood cry
Loud to the listening sky,
Lest it breed riot,
Their money spent
On careful print
Will keep it quiet,
Disguise its flavor
For their breakfast newspaper.

Lie still, you dead,
Wrapped in the heavy bed;
Lie cold and meek.
Your graves possess
In decent humbleness;
They will not hear you speak.
The living speak your word
And will be heard.

(*April 28, 1939*)

Here in the City[11]

All night the streets
lie thick with light;
all night the city streets run up and down
carrying the summer's heat;
all night the slap of feet

11. First published in *New Masses* 40 (July 8, 1941): 20.

repeats incessantly along the street.
The crowded heat climbs up the tenement,
fingers the sleeper's dream.

At nine o'clock the child asked for a drink of water.
At ten o'clock the child, its hair flat with sweat,
whimpered, woke, and asked for a drink of water.
The mother saw prickly heat on its arms and legs,
pushed the bed a little nearer the window.

At one o'clock the child, its eyelids twitching,
woke and saw its mother's naked breast
and father's sleeping nostrils clutch at air,
wanted a drink, cried a little, slept again,
dreaming of melons. All night the heat
sat on the fire-escape. It was a pretty child,
blue eyes in smudges of shadow.

All night the flies
sizzled upward from the garbage pails
ranked along the alley to salute the dawn.
Out of the river to the eastward morning
came with a rattle of milk cans and a breath of air;
the early truck squealed in the street's emptiness.

The child woke in the asphalt-colored sunlight
and all the English sparrows sang together.

(*June* 1939)

Religious Education

Children are betrayed so many ways;
staled by the flies at the corner of the eyelid,
sold to the poolroom, eaten by the slum,
left to the typhoid and the fire. Children

have no weapon, carry no union card,
walk on no picket line around the millionaire
who got the playground closed.

And so he sleeps
on a sweet pillow, builds the model prison
empty and expectant of the new bad boys;
for which they may forgive him if they choose.

But the good boys,
the flesh unspoiled, the useful innocence,
the fine bricks of the future universe;
but the good boys with their round holy eyes
coming to school their mouths sweet with communion:

The Brothers told me General Franco[12] was right,
the Brothers wouldn't tell me if it weren't so.

Brothers of all men brothers of the bomb
in that pure brotherhood where guns and Moors
spread temporary rightness over Spain
and most enduring death; good men who leave
the spittle of lying kisses on the young mouth,
be merry with the dice, the seamless garment,
and waste no time in hoping for the voice:
Forgive the Brothers who know not what they do.[13]

(June 1939)

12. Francisco Paulino Hermenegildo Teódulo Franco Bahamonde (1892-1975) was
general and leader of the Nationalist forces that overthrew the Spanish republic
during the Spanish Civil War; after the war he effectively ruled Spain until his death.
    13. An ironic allusion to Luke 23:34: "Then said Jesus, Father, forgive them; for they
know not what they do. And they parted his raiment, and cast lots."

Dirge for the Suicides[14]
(*In Memory of Ernst Toller*[15])

Be kind to them, love them and give them praise,
forgive them. It was not their fingers
knotted the rope. Forgive them;
it was not their hearts bred the heartsickness
scattered the poison in the concentration camp.
These our brothers have been betrayed to death
who sat in their own skulls and gave directions;
the bullet through the watching eye.

No man is defeated;
he breaks himself, he cuts his strength in pieces,
abjures the fanfare and the parade of dying
to slip out in humility through the back door.
Forgive the easy and untroubled dead
whose hearts broke under exile, whose breath failed,
whose arteries refused to carry blood
into the sadness of the brain. Pardon
the gas-filled flat, the sweet green Cuban waters,
the man alone at lunchtime in the hotel room
swung from the transom of the door. Bury with honor
the courage grown sleepy after years of fighting,
the body gone to sleep.

The living fighters
bear wreaths of forgiveness to the sorry tomb

---

14. First published in *Seven Poets in Search of an Answer*, 32-33.

15. Ernst Toller (1893-1939) was a Polish Jew, poet, playwright, socialist revolutionary, and political activist. Haunted by his nightmarish experiences fighting in the trenches during World War I, he came to believe it was his duty as a human being to write political poetry, primarily in protest against the machinations of repressive governments. He became active in left-wing politics in Germany during the 1920s and early 1930s. After Hitler and the Nazis came to power, he fled to London in 1933. He eventually came to America; depressed and disillusioned, he hanged himself in a New York hotel room on May 22, 1939.

of him who let himself be starved to death,
died in the flophouse; of the unable poet
not suited to grub for life in the dust with his hands.
And we, in difficult and narrow comfort,
cling to the butter on our crust of bread
in desperate arrogance, sharpen our teeth
gnawing the leather from the outworn shoe;
get clubbed in the strike, faint in the demonstration,
manage to exist under the airplane bombs,
only do not die in our black moment
between the bang of three and four o'clock at night
knotting our own defeat about our throats.

(Enemies
boast of this murder, boast they got consent,
the victim gracefully withdrew in honor
of the admirable Coughlin[16] salesman in Times Square;
the murdered man bowed to history. Enemies
boast that when the fire was fierce enough
the burning martyr screamed.

But enemies
go on living, eat pleasantly at banquets;
the suicide bought nothing with his death.)

The newspapers report our comrade died
sliced from living men by the slow knives
of twenty years' defeat. No man is defeated;
the blood runs and the broken body cries;
the spirit sits impregnable in arches of bone
till the spine breaks. Defeat is from within;
the treacherous sickness of the beaten mind.
Forgive the martyr for his martyrdom,

16. Charles Edward Coughlin (1891-1979), better known as Father Coughlin, was a
Roman Catholic priest who developed one of the first deeply loyal mass audiences
in radio broadcast history during the 1930s. The magazine he founded, *Social Justice*,
attacked communism, Wall Street, and Jews.

the narrow bones, the brittle heart strings snapped
by some mere centuries of intolerable pain;
forgive the man who let himself be murdered
by forty thieves.

But kill the thieves;
pile up the bodies of the murderers;
beat no retreat from the interminable battlefield;
suffer the spitting and the leather belts, but live;
wash your hands in pain, but live, but live.

(June 1939)

Pacific Shore[17]

What do we do now?
What do we do now?
Slice the seabeach open with the plough,
salt our tears with the seawater,
seed with our bodies the unpregnant sea?
What do we do now?
Plant our bodies in the ebb and flow?
Harvestless man, wife and son and daughter,
bury ourselves in the nice cheap water?

Where do we go from here?
O pioneer?
Where have we got to go?
What have we got to do?
Shoved off the earth, where do we go from here,
to what clean homestead in what heavenly sphere?
We stand on the nation's edge; our shadows fall
starved lean on the unprofitable wave.

17. First published in *New Masses* 39 (March 25, 1941): 24. In one of the typescript drafts of this poem, Davidman appends: "To John Steinbeck."

Remembering the spilled honey of our days
we see the last land farmed, the field fenced in,
the mountain gold stopping the banker's tooth;
between the fences and the barren sand
is not room for one man to make a stand,
one seed to grow, the scratch of one bird's foot,
the six feet of one grave.

And we, and we
here at the money's end and the work's end
help the sun go down to burial;
sunken in a pit of whispering sand,
claw with our fingers at the sliding wall,
hope to get out this coming year.

Brothers, where do we go from here?
Tell us the road we take from here,
farmer, butcher, baker, beggarman, thief,
doctor, lawyer, Indian chief —

Rich man, where do we go from here?
Give us a ditch to pioneer!

Turn around and take it back again,
turn again and take the country back
that the bank nibbled in the honest man's track;
here's what we do, the road we've got to take;
turn around and help the daylight break,
see stretch naked to the rising sun
the whole new continent, the ungardened land,
the barbed-wire paradise for the fertile gun,
the stripped and beautiful miles, the place for pioneering:

Turn back, turn back our faces to the sun.

(Los Angeles, June 1939)

Easter Greeting

Now returning spring revives
The almond-blossom and the sun,
The warm wind and the leaves
And the cold gun.

Now the simultaneous grass
Glitters on the ground again,
A color good to grace
The blood of men.

Shattering the frosty night,
Spring roars out of the cannon's breath;
O sun, put forth your light,
Adorn our death.

(June 1939)

Hic Jacet[18]

Now we come home with daily pay
Safe from the welter of this day;
Earners of the miracle
Of gold to eat and silk to wear,
Stuff the whispering keyhole well,
Turn down the bedspread, brush the hair,
Lock the poor world out with sleep;
Let no hurt assail the head
Smug with comfort in its bed;
Never smell of hunger creep
Through the perfumes of our sleep.

Stiff upon the frozen dark
Hungry men in silhouette

18. The title is Latin for "here lies."

Make a picture to forget;
Strewn like paper in the park
Flesh and bones and troubles lie
Guarded by the staring sky.
May their eyes assault us never;
May they be locked out forever.

Keep their fingers from our meat;
Do not let them walk our street;
Do not let their crying come
Through the cold and hollow air
Waking us with loud despair;
Do not let them beat the drum
Cruel and sudden in our dreams;
Choke their breath, conceal their screams,
Do not let us hear them weep.
Now we lay us down to sleep.

(July 1939)

Dog's Hour

At the edge of Europe, the last shelf of light,
Seething like flies over the steamer's dock,
Taking the boat at the dog's hour of night,
We listen for the single stroke of the clock,

The spang[19] and rattle of the rising sun;
Take turns keeping ears against the ground
For the first tickle of a distant gun,
The aeroplane's premonitory sound.

Captain, get us seaward through the foam;
The bright hotels are closed, the colored maps

19. A jerk or sudden movement.

Flicker with earthquake, and we must be home
To send them ships loaded with iron scraps.

(*September 7, 1939*)

Ghost Story

Old man, ugly man,
why do you follow me?

Home from the sunset,
out with the morning,
why do you wait
at the street's turning
for my going out
and my returning,

queer one, quiet one,
with your eyes burning?

(*October 1939*)

Sonnets for Proteus[20]

I
This iron gentleman, this unhappy man
Once passed by me savoring the dark air;
He might as well have got his heavy hands
Bodily on my throat as bend his head
At such a dangerous angle to my peace;
He might as well have chained me by the hair
As chain me to the memory of his face
Till I settle down in the final bed.

---

20. In Greek mythology Proteus was a sea or river god, who, like the fluid nature of water, could change his shape. He was sometimes referred to as the Old Man of the Sea.

Therefore, in this corner of the sun,
I keep busy at a statue of him,
Snapping the hasty minutes as they run,
Casting his body in the immortal flame,
Until I have compelled the unripe metal
Into this iron incorruptible.

II

I will not yoke him in an iron collar,
Trap him in silver of the winter's color;
I shall lay no solid name to him.
He is not of one kind or one feature,
Being of the nature of seawater,
Laid out beneath the light in gay or grim,
With the moon changing, in the moonlight's tether,
Shining underneath the wind and weather.

Iron is too bitter for my love
Who does not love the sword's taste on my tongue;
Barren silver; eaten bronze; dead gold;
I shall embrace him in the fugitive
Ripple of sliding sea no arms can hold,
Tasting the salt seawater all night long.

III

Here at his heart the empty iron room
Rang to my question cruel as a bell;
His spirit left me in the watery gloom
Here, without a sign or syllable.
Spirit, spirit, stoop upon my hand;
Spirit, be the iron idol's guest;
Give me his heavy breast upon my breast
In the dark night, in the dark foreign land.

I am betrayed; evaded; he is fled.
His painted mouth is dry upon the wall.
There is no honor in this counterfeit

To do the service that I need of it;
For I will have incarnate in my bed
His lips, his eyes, his body, bones, and all.[21]

(November 28, 1939)

Coldwater Canyon[22]

The bird that sang to us some time ago,
blue, seawater blue, kingfisher blue,
has got so draggled in the heavy snow
the glory has gone out of him; still

still he comes crying, still the birdsmouth music
shabbily pipes us out across the winter,
still the blood answers in the heart's pipes,
speaks in the eardrum, tingles in the fingers.

Nevertheless these bones make a sorry show
clattering in the winter wilderness,
walking into sun out of this forest of darkness,
pride for their cover, manskin for their dress;

nor has life got any use for us;
we are not good servants in our stained clothing;
we are not fit for torches in his house
illuminated with the fire of loving.

21. Davidman appends this note at the end of the poem: "Coldwater Canyon, Night."

22. First published in Accent: A Quarterly of New Literature 2 (Summer 1941): 200. This poem appears to have been written just as Davidman was leaving Hollywood and her failed attempt at screenwriting. Very much in the tradition of a valediction, it is her resigned good-bye to all that she disliked about and all that thwarted her during her stay in Hollywood.

Only let nothing cry us up again,
no bird, no honor, no awakening drum;
let us go peaceably among the dead men,
safe into darkness out of the abyss of sun.

(December 5, 1939)

Everytown

Skyward the deflected wind
off the radio tower is blown;
never shall one find
silence in that town;

stranger, in these parts
never hope for rest,
but the angry heart
knocking in the breast.

In the rattling wilderness,
stranger, to get by
never ask for quietness;
quiet men die,

gentle men go under
in the drowning mist;
comrade, ask for thunder
and the clenched fist.

(December 19, 1939)

For the Gentlemen[23]

When you see red
it will be too late;
the night will be dead,
the sun will not wait;
say, can you see
what the sunrise will be?

When you command
the sea to stand still
at the safe edge of sand,
do you think that it will?
say, do you know
where the high tide will go?

Call for your cannon,
call for your drum,
buzz with the aeroplane,
burst with the bomb;
you're up a tree now;
say, while you rave,
say, can you see now
the depth of your grave?

(December 1939)

Observation in Kansas

Seeing the light fall on America
slantwise out of an icy sky; seeing
the blunt-headed cattle nosing for grass
in this stubble, in these brittle pastures;

23. First published in *New Masses* 38 (December 31, 1940): 23. Davidman later published this poem under the title "For the Nazis" in *Seven Poets in Search of an Answer*, 34.

shall not a man ask; where has it gone,
the green fullness and the wealthy rain
used to breed flowers on this naked plain?

Where has it gone, the green grass
that had the habit of blessing these pastures?
Where has the water gone; the gold water
that we loved, that was stinging sweet
in the mouth, in the thirsty wheat,
that carried rainbow trout, that the sun played in,
when we were boys we used to wade in?

Who sucked the water out of the earth's cups,
cut the trees and let the water run
naked to the unrelenting sun?
Who bought up the trees in the cheap market,
got his hands on the land and grubbed the roots up;
who tore up the farmhouse from the ground
like the way the twister spins it round,
ate the people from it, let it drop
empty, the house for wind to rattle in
from Oklahoma up to Michigan?

Whom have we got to thank for this,
the duststorm and the tumbleweed's kiss,
the dead corn and the living sand
over the place we plowed our land
straight in the furrow?
                  whom have we to thank
but the gentleman in the brass cage at the bank
locked in with dollars; purified with glass;
drying up the cattle and the grass?

Brother, the axe is falling in this hour
and under it had better be the neck
of someone answerable for this wreck.
Here in the barren field we break our backs,

claw the dear water from the desert cracks:
brother, whose neck is underneath the axe?
But if the water's gone and the land's gone
don't blame it on the weather or the stars;
don't blame it on the foreign trick of wars,
don't blame it on the government or God
trying to whip us virtuous with his rod;
blame it on men, the men, the gentlemen
no bigger than us, no brighter or braver than us,
and, by the Eternal, much less dangerous![24]

(December 21, 1939)

I Have My Pride

Abominable pain and denatured bread
are what I get, or burning wake and watch
stars in their processional fine march
nightly; while you remain alive. I wish

you had to lie so; stare at night so; twitch,
want to undress yourself of flesh and blood;
or, since I cannot get you in my bed,
I wish you would lie down among the dead;

I am wild to cut your body open
with broken glass, bury you deep in slime,
stamp on your drowning face. O I would use
the cruelest fire and most envenomed weapon.
My love, my love; there never was a time
you could not have my soul to wipe your shoes.

(1939?)

24. Davidman appends this note to the end of the poem: "For the Kansas girl on the train." This suggests that she wrote the poem on her return train trip from Hollywood to New York.

Ballade of a Roll in the Hays[25]

We are the writers of Hollywood!
Hear us gurgle and gulp and gush;
Watch our heroes wade through blood,
Lookit our heroines wallow in plush!
We are masters of moony mush,
Creative artists, and how it pays!
Take those clothes off Crawford[26] ... hush,
Remember it's got to get past Will Hays![27]

All our wives are misunderstood,
All our cuties are oh, so lush;
If we wrote Little Red Riding Hood
We'd have her meet with wolf with a rush;
A wolf in the bed is worth two in the bush!
Be subtle, boys, there are ways and ways ...
Frinstance, Hedy in "Ecstasy"[28] — shushhh,
Remember it's got to get past Will Hays!

How it hurts that we've got to be good,
Dealers in lukewarm slime and slush!
We've got hair on our chests, we could ...
(Censored to spare the goils a blush) ...
In our apelike arms we'd crush
Oomph girls like heroes of Hemingway's;[29]

25. The ballade is a verse form that consists of three eight-line stanzas, each with a consistent meter and a particular rhyme scheme; the last line in the stanza is a refrain. Ballades end with an envoi, a four-line concluding stanza.

26. Joan Crawford (1904-1977), born Lucille Fay LeSueur, was a famous American film actress; she won an Oscar in 1945.

27. William Harrison Hays, Sr. (1879-1954), was the first president of the Motion Picture Producers and Distributors of America (1922-1945). His chief legacy was the creation of The Motion Picture Production Code, or the Hays Code, the set of industry moral censorship guidelines that governed the production of most films released by American film studios from 1930 to 1968.

28. Hedy Lamarr (1914-2000) starred in the 1933 film *Ecstasy*.

29. Ernest Miller Hemingway (1899-1961) was one of the most important American novelists of the first half of the twentieth century.

Greta Garbo,[30] ve loff you so mosh!
— Remember it's got to get past Will Hays!

L'Envoi
Prince, while we write for a baritone thrush,
An infant canary, our art decays!
We are organizing a PUTSCH!!![31]
Remember, it's got to get past Will Hays!

(1939?)

Elegy for the New Year

We together, being children of this winter,
the black night of year when the frost comes,
seeing the roof shake and the window splinter
at the reverberation of the bombs;

we, being together in this year
appraised by the captains in the slave market
for employment in the uses of war,
the gun's manservant and its fancy target;

let us swallow our last breath of air,
hold a celebration in our house,
kiss the wife goodbye upon the stair
till the last minute that the law allows,

then by necessity to the sweet slaughter;
holes in the turning earth delay for us;
harlot, lover, mother, wife, and daughter,
pope, priest, politician, pray for us.

(January 1, 1940)

---

30. Greta Garbo (1905-1990), born Greta Lovisa Gustafsson, was a Swedish film actress who at this time was an international star and Hollywood icon.
31. A violent revolution.

See the Pretty Skywriting

The white and silent sky they give us
For our habitable tent
Mysteriously brays above us
Luxurious advertisement:

lie down, lie down, my customer;
plop in your open mouth do reach
for very small expenditure
the nectarine and curious peach;

apples of the Hesperides
plump your skin with vitamins!
The sunless bottom of the seas
sprout pearls and unctuous fins,

so gold the world and full of juice
to grace your table. Come, disburse;
open your hungry jaws, unloose
the iron latches of your purse.

Sweetly we perish in our ditch
When we can feast our frozen eyes
On the immortal words that preach
Of savory banquets in the skies.

(February 1940)

Dayspring[32]

What of the night!
The stars are fastened
in their old place, tight and glistening;

32. First published in *New Masses* 39 (June 17, 1941): 17.

the earth is pinned
with its old pin;
the moon's in place,
half dark, half bright.

So far so good.
What of the night?
The lights work
if you press the switch,
the poor are poor,
the rich are rich.
As for God,
that's as you prefer;
the sick child groans,
death throttles her.
The sleeper turns
from left to right;

the world spins over.
What of the night?

Ask in the subways
how many seats
give you a place for your head
and one for your feet.
Sleep in the middle
on your belly sits,
telling it lies about
how full it is.
Ask the grass
how you make your bed,
what newspapers keep
the light from your head:

Not so good.
What of the night?
Why, they take gas,

they take to drink,
they sleep on the grass,
they wake and think.
The wars can go on
Just as well as in the daylight,
the searchlights manage it.
This is progress;
if you have doubt,
better banish it;
for safety keep
to prudent sleep.

What of the night?
Nothing very much.
The rich hold tight
with a nervous clutch.
The poor let life go
by inches; death
does a good business
sucking up breath
and exploiting heartbreaks.
The sound you hear
is the noise that pain makes.
Nothing very much
to report of the night.
Only, eastward,
Notice the light.

(February 1940)

Success Story

girlie girlie girlie said the producer
in this business you gotta gotta gotta
give give give if you want to be a star
shine in the sky and own a private bar

so the blonde let down her hair
stepped shrinking out of her underwear
and in due course of time all sorts of honor
not to mention gelt[33] was heaped upon her,
and when she went swimming in her private pool
her long hair floated on the water behind her
like dreams, like seaweed, like mist,
only much more often kissed:

for ten years she Rapunzel Melusina[34]
the water fairy waggled her breasts in front of
American men from seven to seventy-seven
and what was left of the European market,
marrying and being given in marriage
four times to what the studio could scrape up to
     cover her shame
with the aid of the fashionable abortionist

Nevertheless and in spite of precautions taken
other younger breasts enraptured the attentive eyes of
the bald-headed perspiring man who took it out in
     fan letters
and Rapunzel with her hair a little specious
started doing mother parts
              and who cared
then or when they fished her from the water,
Melusina with her hair all curly
and the tongues clucking girlie girlie girlie?

                    (February 1940)

33. Money.

34. Melusina appears as a beautiful, supernatural female in a number of folktale motifs; she is often portrayed as a mermaid, the sense in which Davidman uses her in this poem.

Spring Dance

When the clouds come howling over this water
be sure the aeroplanes will stay at home;
they will not risk getting their wings wet
loosing bombs to taint the clear drink of air;
they will sit indoors and comb their hair.

Wait for the summer, women, wait for the grass
and the green days, wait for the silver fire
of the sun's breath making the heart glad.
The neat eagles with sunfire on their wings
will stop above us:
                    we shall take fright,
go plunging down the stairway into night
signaled to us by the stoppage of our breath.

When the sky distempers and goes black
is it the night falling or the roof falling,
is it sanctuary, sleep, or death?
Huddle together, women, in the cellar,
while the world goes crash above our heads,
breaking up our kitchens and our beds;

huddle together, each take the other's hand
for warmth and for peace of mind in the
tumultuous rat's nest of obscurity;
somewhere the bells ring, somewhere the rain rings
cleaning the tenantless air.

                    But where we are lying
the roots of things go by us in the dark,
well fattened, and exfoliate overhead
propped by our bones and on our marrow fed,
nor shall resurrection day suffice to get us up
from under the tumble of steel where our house was
and where season after season we are so quiet.

So we are patient for summer and the new grass
and the new sun and the new eagles flying.

(February 1940)

For the Happy Man[35]

You have gone swimming naked in the night time
with no light but the half light of the moon;
you have laughed into the invisible water,
kissed the waves as they came to meet you.

Do you remember how good it is
kissing the water's lip,
afterward diving into sleep
sheets and blankets, warmth and peace?

You remember all the evenings, you
remember the games and the singing and the love;
they are good things for any man to have.
Give them to us all, we want them too.

(February 1940)

Off the Record

If I could slip my body's noose,
if I could turn my bones to air,
have the wind's wings upon my shoes
and braids of lightning in my hair,

I should assume a falling star's
quicksilver leap from sea to sea

---

35. First published in *New Masses* 38 (February 18, 1941): 36.

above the continental bars
that separate my love and me,

and find him in the final hills,
and creep like moonlight on his house,
and pass between the doors and sills
through cracks too narrow for a mouse.

(February 1940)

Affectionately Yours

Nobody says enough for men like you,
Nobody cares to love the quiet ones
Who will not love themselves, nobody dares
To praise you to your faces; only once
I saw one of you walking the night's edge,
Little brother of the moons and suns.

And he was far away behind the hedge
Of his impenetrable reticence;
To worship would have been to give offense.

Nobody has been quick enough to get
Hands upon his walking silhouette;
Let me try to catch him in my words,
The silent man, entangled in a net
Fragile as the silence of the birds.

(March 1940)

Prophet without Honor[36]

You man standing on the mountaintop,
what do you see that's worth the climb up?

You get stiff eyelashes, you get a taste
of snow in your mouth, and a bath of mist;

the hard wind blows you deaf and blind;
what do you see that's worth the climb,
what have you got that we have missed?

If you come down to us and say
there's nothing more than everyday
over the hills and far away,

nothing to think we have not thought,
no novelties in tears and laughter,
no fight that we have never fought,
nothing before and nothing after;

if you come down and tell us this
you'll buy our love, you'll buy our kiss.

But if not, if you stand and stare
over the sky to bluer air,
we'll crucify you standing there.

(*March* 1940)

It Is Later than You Think

Minutes are slipping past you while you speak;
If you try to get your hooks on one

36. First published in *New Masses* 38 (January 14, 1941): 14.

You will find it simply can't be done.
Never was a man yet who could make
Time sit down and talk to him and take
Notice of his presence; though they say
Joshua made the sun stand still one day.[37]
But that was probably the sun's mistake.

Minutes trickle by you when you wait
And when you stop waiting and hurry and try
To grab a few of them before you die.
Remember it is always getting late;
Meanwhile time marches on, and you are in it.
Minutes are whistling past you every minute.

(*March* 1940)

Incubus, Incubus![38]

You, sir, were you not troubled in your sleep
Night before last, were you not broad awake
And staring hard into the empty dark?
It was I who whispered in your ear.
It is I that you must always fear
When you turn the light out, when you creep
Into sanctuary, when you take
Refuge from me in your sacred bed;
You will find me standing by its head.

This must be the way of things with you
Until you learn that there is no escape
From the ominous and deadly shape
That holds a knife to cut your sleep in two.
Study what it is you have to do.

(*March* 1940)

---

37. Davidman alludes here to the biblical story found in Joshua 10:12-14.

38. An incubus was a legendary evil demon who would secretly steal upon a person in order to have sexual relations. The name is derived from the Latin "to lie upon."

The House of Last Resort

The man who owned the skeleton
That smiles at me so pleasantly
Went walking underneath the sun,
And he was very good to see:

He wore his bones so near the skin,
I found it not impossible,
Only by using my eyes on him,
To feel the angles of his skull;

He was unseemly quick to die.
He should have waited for my love
To pump new blood into him. I
Have enough, and more than enough;

So I went out and brought him home,
Late, late one shiny bitter night.
He was too good to leave alone
Once the worms had cleaned him white;

Here he keeps me company,
Here he sits him down to rest.
I have locked my heart with a golden key
Into the cage that was his breast.

(June 1940)

When the Sun Came Up

When the sun came up
we did not let him look.
Who gave him the right
to handle the sky's gold?
Light and starlight

were not meant for him;
so we locked the world
and did not let him in.

Hoard your kindness
for your own need,
all the wise men said;
it is precious stuff.
You have not heart enough
to go around;
if he asks for love,
shove him underground.

So when night shut
tight over the house,
we left him outside
to look through our windows.
Secure indoors
in our comfort and pride,
we are healthy and virtuous.
Why does he hate us?

(June 1940)

Unknown Soldier

Visiting ghosts must carefully walk lightly
since it is your nerves on which they step
when they open up the window nightly
and intrude their death upon your sleep;
ghosts if they want your pardon must take care
that on your heart they weigh as little as air.

Nevertheless he, walking out of his bones,
twilight, unimportant, discreate,
floating in a semifluid state

overhead, can weigh as much as stones
that ceremoniously they piled upon
his spilt blood to keep his spirit down.

(July 1940)

Game with Children[39]

Come now, let us be tigers,
let us be tigers walking in the jungle
under the leaves where the green dew lingers
quietly, where nothing comes with guns.

Nothing is strong enough to hurt tigers;
see how they walk, shaking the dew from the leaves;
let us be proud tigers in the cool evening
stepping as softly as a man breathes.

Tigers eat big dinners every day,
after which they always go to sleep
sweetly underneath the shining palm trees.
No one makes a noise to wake them up;
men have no bombs, they have only a spear.
Children, children, let us go away and be tigers.

(July 1940)

39. First published in Accent: A Quarterly of New Literature 2 (Summer 1941): 200-201.

Dirge for Western Civilization

This house is as dark as the belly of a gun;
Open the windows and let in the sun.

> The carpets' colors will quiver and fade
> Brought face to face with the sun's fusillade.

This house is musty with solemn old sin;
Open the doors and let the wind in.

> The crystal will break with a crash on the floor
> If the wind walks in through our front door.

This house is a grave of immoderate size;
Body of man, arise, arise!

(September 1940)

The Suspense Is Terrific

How we dare enjoy our minor love
Under the wings of this enormous death
I cannot understand. We are not brave;
Terror pierces us, pain steals our breath.
Still, in the night, we kiss and have our smile.
Meanwhile the earth turns round and the wheels move
Us closer to our inevitable grave
Under the bombs. Let us lie still awhile,

Lie still, and taste the flavor of this fruit,
Bittersweet pulp beneath the searching tongue.
Sniff the sweet wind and listen to the song
Of uninstructed birds; one minute yet
Before the doorbell rings and the guns shoot
And we, whom the gods do not love, die young.

(September 1940)

Fugue

Discontented winter
and a stormy spring
splashing rainy silver
over the birds' singing;

out of this window
in the walls of life
I stepped into
the mysterious river

of flowering air
at the world's edge;
when I got there
he had gone further.

In the silences
between the symphonies,
in the soft abysses
between the neat trees,

in the air-bubbles
under the sea,
in geometric scribbles
of infinity,

where the world has no face
and the sun no name,
he has built his palace
of immortal flame.

(September 1940)

Neant[40]

Hang up your empty body on a hook,
the stars advised him.
                    And the moonlight said
you will be part of us when you are dead.
Tie your rope tightly around your neck.

For innumerable years it was his curse
to see and not to be the universe.
He would have liked to let it swallow him
with the huge gullet of the vacuum;

but, when in pious haste to be enrolled
in that dead immortal company,
he took the rope and did as he was told,
the moon shut its windows and the stars blinked out,
and there was nothing anywhere about;

nothing anywhere, not even he.

(September 1940)

Moral Lesson

Melodious oriole,
go dig yourself a hole
to hide your innocence.
If you had any sense
you would not sing.

Why are you not afraid?
Concealed beneath the leaf
teeth in the serpent's head

---

40. The title means nothingness or emptiness.

anticipate your death.
If you knew anything;

if you were wise like us,
you would forever wear,
on your black and golden face,
golden and black despair.
Look at the human race.

We hold our kingly place
as your superior,
mellifluous oriole,
by virtue of our fear.
Go dig yourself a hole,
and from bird turn mole.

(September 1940)

Bitter Medicine

Out of the eastern ocean's cup,
washed about with nightly gloom,
I lap the harsh seawater up
under the inconstant moon,

the constant moon, the doublefaced
starlady that I met last year,
smiling equivocal and chaste
over the west the same as here.

Seawater tastes the same as blood
by eastern or by western sea;
the moon is neither bad nor good
with only one of us to see;

and I am here, and he is there;
and you are privileged to hear

a tidy statement of despair;
he is there, and I am here.

It would be easier to love
a buried man, and waste my breath
asking for favors of the grave;
there's no uncertainty in death.

(October 1940)

Echo

From knocking my fists against a wall
I have worn them down to skin
and bone so miserably thin
they do not stop the light at all.

My empty veins have let it drip,
the blood that should be locked up tight;
passageways for air and light
run from my heart to my fingertip.

Light, light; the bright devouring sun,
the vicious day have tattered me
till there is nothing left to see
but the ghost of my skeleton.

What should I do now but rejoice
to be, instead of clumsy clay,
a thing you cannot drive away;
only a voice, only a voice?

(October 1940)

Incidental Music

Man, do you not hear the drum?
It is my heart that raps within
the birdcage breast; for when you come
my blood rings underneath my skin,
and the universe around
trills and trembles with the sound.

Man, do you not see the fire?
I have lit it with my flesh.
Such a blaze is called desire;
soon it must be fed afresh.
It will be another sun
with your bones to batten on.

Images are not enough;
I am honest in my love.
I will have, and have, and have
all your body for my slave;
I will burn you through and through.
Let me get my hands on you.

(October 1940)

Trojan Women[41]

In the smoke and screaming air
they got across the bridges with their children,
carrying their household gods and silverware.
The waters boiled with submarines,
and the clouds boiled with planes.

41. First published in Accent: A Quarterly of New Literature 2 (Summer 1941): 201. Reprinted in Seven Poets in Search of an Answer, 35-36.

Hurry, hurry;
death flows at your heels like a hissing wave
chasing the children up the sand,
times we went to the beach.
                                Coney Island
was the first place they landed.

Hurry, hurry;
don't be looking back over your shoulder
as at the new moon in an empty sky
to make a wish;
                        or at a man.
It was a sweet place to love a man in,
the city with the lights and movie houses,
two rooms and kitchenette and frigidaire;
that was where we lived and you could see
the empire state building from the bedroom window
with the sun slick on it all the way up.

And just then
the empire state building made a perfect candle
of explosion and illumination
and burst all the way up;
                                and they looked back
over their hurrying shoulders.

And Troy town
reverberated as the walls came down.   (*November* 1940)

The Virgin and the Swine

There was nothing to tell him my name
except the wind at the windowpane.

There was nothing to show him my face
except the moon in the caves of space.

The talking wind was clear and keen;
it woke him with a silver scream.

The desperate moonlight cried and cried;
but he turned on the other side,

locked ears against the wind's cold shout;
went back to sleep and shut me out.

(December 1940)

Proteus: Because Your Hands Are Only Hands

Because your hands are only hands, because
you move in ugliness and breathe in pain
and you are sure to die like other men,
subservient to nature's dirty laws;

since I am likely to have broken bones
if I fall, and I will always fall;
and since your body too is breakable
as long as flesh is not as hard as stones;

since you are not a god within a star
and I am not a dyad in a tree,
and heaven has no crowns for you and me
and we are no better than we are,

Why, there is nothing left to us, my lover,
except for you and me to hurt each other.

(December 1940)

Proteus: One Takes His Lover by the Hand

One takes his lover by the hand
and through the naked fields of grass
side by side these lovers pass
smiling, hand in equal hand;

one looks downward at his feet
with a stiff unbending head,
and the proud eyes in his head
see his lover at his feet;

I, thrown down upon my knees,
take the abominable weight
and never after stand up straight,
crawling to love on hands and knees.

(*December 1940*)

To Follow You Around

To follow you around New York
snooping from behind each tree
keeps me from doing any work;
it is not sensible of me.

How many nights I lay awake
and watched the passing autos shake
their lights against the bedroom wall,
with heavy eyelids for your sake.

How many times I saw the ball
of the moon spring up and fall,
ticking the seasons of my pain,
those nights I could not sleep at all.

(*December 1940*)

This and That...

Fold yourself up in darkness; hide
out of the compass of the moon.
Light will not uncover you
naked to the addled view;
dress yourself in heavy night
to defend you from my sight.

Close the walls about your head,
sealed within an airtight room.
Cower underneath the bed.
If these tricks are not enough
to protect you from my love,
you can always try a tomb.

Nevertheless and nevertheless
I am certain to possess
your fine soul and body too
and the sound of your least breath.
You have nothing that will do
to keep my clever hands from you,
not even death, not even death.

    we are the rotten men,
    the intellectuals
    who have instead of brain
    money in their skulls;

    Behind our bolted door
    life smells good;
    we send men off to war
    and rhyme the blood.

There never was anyone I loved who
did not leave me naked in the rain
and nasty wind. There never was

anyone I loved who did not sooner or later
throw me out into the sneering night;
there never was a man I loved who didn't
treat me to every sort of misery;
and that is, I suppose, as it should be;
that's what I do to people who love me.

(*December* 1940)

Litany for War

For my laughter, for my laughter, for my life,
for the pleasure of my bed,
for my daily eating bread,
for feeling comfortable, feeling safe;

for not being strong enough
to enforce upon this world
an inexorable love;
for having failed
to free these slaves,

and listening to the guns,
and seeing what is done,
and liking to draw breath,
forgive me, graves.

Forgive me for consenting in your death.
Forgive me for smearing my words over your death.

(1940)

Good Advice

I
They never answer you, they never answer;
never mind how many bells you ring
that say their name with ding and dong and ding
dong; the cat's in the well. For they are drowned
in the dim bath of time. Do not
go ringing bells that never make a sound.
If all you love has earth inside its eyes,
why, let love lie quiet where it lies;

they have their use now and their frozen purpose:
to breed the summer green. If they came back
they would not walk with any kind of grace
under the sun. Grass would not like their tread.
Child, the living are hard enough to wake;
do not go mad trying to wake the dead.

II
When you stand up
out of your mother's womb,
till you hit the tomb
do not sleep.

Stretch your eyes wide.
Stare from side to side.
Gentle water laps
smiling at your feet.
Water likes to eat.
Watch your step.

Look out for daylight!
she knows how to bite.
Hold your breath
when you walk at night.
Night has teeth.

Fly, fly
from the enormous sky.

When your long disease
consents to be over,
you will have peace
and a cosy cover.
The world's a safe bed
only for the dead.

(1940?)

Dirge for a Dead Appeaser

What is left
let the wind's
cold fingers sift.

Let the wind scatter
tongue and limb
and all of him.
Does it matter?

Let rain dissolve
with its cold love
what the wind spares.
And who cares?

(December 1940?)

Idiot's Song

I saw a rainbow
bent above a plain;
I guessed I would go
through the dripping rain

till I came where
the rainbow took root,
and stood and stared
at gold in a pot,

and ran home with gold
stuck to my fingers.
I walked through the cold
weather's stinging

to the rainbow's end
in the empty plain.
What should I find
but the dripping rain?

(*December* 1940?)

By All Means Let Us Have Truth

By all means let us have truth
since we have nothing to lose;
accept the envenomed tooth
and deflowered rose.
Honesty, honesty!
Let us take off our clothes.

First truth; I saw a man
and called him loving names.
I never did see you;
your body blocked the view.
I blocked it with sweet dreams,
and you with eyes and hands
not quite like other men.
I did not love you, then.

Second; I saw myself
in the mirror of your eye,

and that was what I wanted.
I loved the loving glass,
self by self enchanted.
I kissed my kissing face
and never looked behind
to where the secret mind
sat in your skull alive.
You I did not love.

This is all quite true;
that is the way it was.
I shall not attempt to deny
the comfortable lie.
I have washed myself white
from any touch of yours,
and I might sleep at night
if you would only die.[42]

(1940?)

Always or Never Tell the Truth

Always or never tell the truth;
always to the true man; species ruthless
in the brain's use, unyielding
to soft sweet loving nonsense that sustains
instead of brains.

Always or never.

Always to the accuser doubter devil
der Geist der stets verneint,[43] the unburied

---

42. In Davidman's hand she appends this note to the poem: "For an early love who was not my love."

43. This is from a line spoken by Mephistopheles in Goethe's *Faust*: "I am the spirit

unsleeping adversary of the smug,
who will not cling to Papa overhead
that takes you into heaven when you're dead,
who will not pat the stars upon the head
and himself their baby, will not lie
into the inexorable eye
of the microscope.
                  This is the true man;
he can take truth in his flesh and bone,
the arrow, the immedicable pain.

Never tell the truth to anyone
who cannot bear it; who would like to know
God loves him, there is neither fire nor snow,
only jonquils, only Paradise
sweet and green and golden to his eyes:

He is your grandfather, you owe him lies.

                                    (1940?)

Mothlike

Held by some deadly rune
Round you I whirl,
Like that poor lovesick girl,
The constant moon

Around the great earth, who
Will never care
For that pale moony stare;
No more will you.

---

of perpetual negation" (scene 6, line 1338). *Faust, Part One*, trans. David Luke (Oxford: Oxford University Press, 1987).

Nightly I hear her sigh
For loss of liberty;
She never can get free;
No more can I.

(1940?)

Powerful Rhyme: Soon, My Dear, You Will Be Dead

Soon, my dear, you will be dead;
they will put earth above your head,
make a murmur of despair
and go away and leave you there;
your wife will cry, and then your wife
will pick up her daily life
where she dropped it; in a while
she will remember you and smile,
then she will die. And I shall die,
and not be worried if I lie
near you or far; and everyone
who loved your body will be gone,
and everyone who saw your face
will be nourishing the grass
where the tough roots interlace.
No one will be left to care
for your brown face and your gray hair,
no one's memory will dangle
on your jawbone's lovely angle;
your own bones will have forgotten
what they were before they were rotten,
and your name will get no kiss
except for this, except for this.

(1940?)

Pastiche

The daylight and the night together
He follows me from place to place;
In sunset or in stormy weather
I am the steward of his face.

White upon the midnight cloud
He like the horned moon is seen;
All the earth and air are loud
With his singing shrill and keen.

Isis and Orus and the dog
Anubis haste;[44] within my mind
join his shadow in the fog,
of god and not of human kind.

(1940?)

Hopeless Song

If I were a cat
on a quartet of feet,
I could follow you where you go
and not be known;

if I were the weightless
feet of light
I could come into your room;

---

44. In ancient Egypt, Isis was the goddess of the ideal wife and mother; Orus (or Horus) was the falcon-headed deity with whom the Pharaohs identified, believing themselves to be the earthly embodiment of the god; and Anubis was the jackal-headed god of the afterlife.

if I were the wind
I could whistle through your door;

if I were dead
I would not think about you any more.

(1940?)

Poems 1941-1952

Defeatist

Deep down, deep down,
out of sight of the moon,
we lie all night
with our eyes locked tight.

Seas of air
roar overhead;
what do we care
who are safe in bed?

This is so good
a place to sleep in,
we are not afraid
of any man's weapon;

sealed from the sun,
drowsy with ease,
deep down, deep down
we rest in peace.

(January 1941)

For a Second Front

You may be born with
a hole inside your heart;
not a bullet's bite,
and not love's tooth;
a pair of open lips
from which blood drips;

a door you cannot shut
through which death eavesdrops.
You may not die of it;
you may be smiling, but
your blood knows better;
like quicksilver, like water
it will run away.

So our courage runs,
drop by drop, these times.
Better die at once.
Better stand today.

(December 1941?)

Epitaph for Myself

As you grow up they peel you;
first, the child's love;
rain and sun and the doll,
the cherry tree in the backyard,
the taste of chocolate candy
and the movie on Saturday.
Have you got these any more?
They have been taken away.

As you grow up they strip you,

taking off like a smock
the girl's love;
how you trusted your mother,
how you trusted your man,
thinking his eyes God's eyes.
Do you think so any more?

As you grow up they flay you
and drop you on the rubbish heap,
taking the wounds and the kisses,
the way your thoughts made sense,
the way the world did, once;
leaving you only the desire for sleep.

Nothing stirs.
Your heart is dust.

Your womb is dust,
your eyes are frozen.
You are quite dead and the snow has buried you,
and yet, you will go on fighting till the spring.

(Winter 1941-1942)[1]

Convalescence

Grateful for summer and the green trees
and the passionate birds beating their hearts and wings
faster than the clock, I lie
watching the leaves write music on the sky;

concerned with my breathing, see the several ribs
rise and fall together; take the breeze

---

1. Davidman's handwritten note appears at the end of the typescript: "Winter 41-42 when I was sick."

smelling of blueberries and strawberries
deep into the hollow cave of bone.

I am that poet that was dead one time
and have returned, decking my skeleton
again with festoons of spring;
have returned, bringing you this word.
O it is the right shape for your lips:

that buried bones may rise again, that one
lying breathless may take up his bed
and walk, and climb into the tingling sun;
and the slow heart may quicken like a bird,
and the brain make its honey like a hive
of resurrected bees; that you and I
are alive, alive, alive, alive.

(Winter 1941-1942)

Peter the Plowman[2]

All the sunlight fell on all the people,
clashed with the headlights of the motorcars,
battled in brightness with the windowpanes,
poured like an army out of the sky;

attacked the faces, telling
how they hide behind their tightened lips,
and each one glances at the tattling light
and fear sits in the corner of each eye;

and the sunlight was no good to them.
They ran down the street, they were in a hurry
to get back to the shady nook in hell

2. First published in *New Masses* 44 (September 15, 1942): 15.

where they lie down with arms around their worry
in decent privacy. Then I,

I the songmaker, the sun's conscious lover,
had my vision, not in dreamy weather,
nor in lightning nor the burning bush,
but soberly in winter while the sun
lit up the loneliness of everyone;

saw myself and all the songmakers
as hollow bugles to the people's mouth
speaking the Judgment word. I heard
the tombs explode; I saw the dead arise.
I saw fear leave the corners of their eyes;

I was never the flesh, never the spirit.
I was never the speaker nor the spoken
word nor the will nor the puff of breath even,
but through me rolled the everlasting sound
dragging the sleepers up from underground;

Poet, poet, you are the people's trumpet;
golden and clean, put yourself to their lips,
tear yourself apart to shout their word
so that no gun is louder, no fear is louder,
no frightening bell is louder in its steeple;

till all the sunlight shines on all the people.

(1942)

Prayer for Every Voyage[3]

Moontrap sea, let go my man,
stop weaving ripples over his eyes,
stop tying seaweed round his hand,
let him out to talk loud again,

Mantrap sea with the salty teeth
biting holes in my man's ship,
let him have peaceful air to breathe,
let him come home and go to sleep

with my hand lying under his head
and my whisper there to soothe
the dreamwaves galloping over the bed,
make his lips soft and his eyelids smooth.

Deathtrap water, open your door,
let him out to talk loud again,
slash his way through the sea once more
and carry the guns to the fighting men.

(1943)

Fairytale[4]

At night, when we dreamed,
we went down a street,
and turned a corner;
we went down the street
and turned the corner,

3. First published in *New Masses* 47 (April 27, 1943): 16.

4. First published in *War Poems of the United Nations*, ed. Joy Davidman (New York: Dial Press, 1943), 299-300. It also appears in Davidman's autobiographical essay, "The Longest Way Round," *Out of My Bone: Letters of Joy Davidman* (Grand Rapids: Eerdmans, 2009), 89 (hereafter *Bone*).

and there, it seemed,
there was the castle.

Always, if you knew,
if you knew how to go,
you could walk down a street
(the daylight street)
that twisted about
and ended in grass;
there it was
always, the castle.

Remote, unshadowed,
childish, immortal,
with two calm giants
guarding the portal,
stiff in the sunset,
strong to defend,
stood castle safety
at the world's end.

O castle safety,
Love without crying,
honey without cloying,
death without dying!
Hate and heartbreak
all were forgot there;
we always woke,
we never got there.

(1943)

For My Son[5]

That time I climbed our hill in the dark
the moon went climbing up the sky;
I held my breath, I hushed my voice,
walked on the grass to make no noise,
yet all the dogs began to bark
at me and the moon as we came by.

All the dogs of all the shires
barked at me and the shameless moon.
The earth and heaven shone together,
admirable flying weather;
the moonlight almost quenched the fires
where bombs had dropped that afternoon.

She is the lantern of the dead;
the living have put out their lights
and seek a temporary grave.
Only the naked bones are brave.
They do not hide the fleshless head
from the fierce wonder of these nights.

Knife in my belt against a thief,
tune on my lips against a fear,
I waited for their planes to fill
the vacant moonlight on the hill,
trying to be as brave in life
as you were in your death, my dear.

(1943)

5. First published under the pseudonym Megan Coombes-Dawson in *War Poems of the United Nations*, 25.

Four Years after Munich[6]

Overarching now the cathedral of green branches
groined above our heads; intricately
cuts up the sunlight; impossible to see
planes analyze the sky to a network of death;
impossible to hear, otherwise than bees' drone
in sticky limeblossom, the voice of planes;
manifestly impossible impossible
to smell danger in the peace of leaves;

multifoliate fingers
entangle us in blindness
sleep falls from the leaves

Here we consumed our summer in impatience,
waited for the rich harvest home and the autumn colours;
here we hid in the valley of England

O then in winter
the death came over naked England
and we saw clearly; parabola
of tracer bullets lightening darkness
and the searchlight's dirty white
and the final fatal slanting fall of the bombs
and the whole night lit up for understanding.

Now we have learned;
this was waiting in the valley, this
made mouths at us behind the screen of leaves,
the gold and green, the mavis and the merle
in Sherwood forest; this
we would not recognize, fingering the comfortable moment —

6. First published under the pseudonym Haydon Weir in *War Poems of the United Nations*, 49-50. The following note appears at the end of the poem: "Haydon Weir was killed in action in 1942."

clatter of brains in the City, fox's brush,
grouse and salmon, the bun in the ABC,
the picnic papers littering the Heath,
the semi-detached villa, the half-a-loaf
ultimately proved worse than no bread at all.

In this last summer
we see clearly; no longer
the summer banners of the trees as bright as ever
serve for concealment.
We part them with armed hands and stare at the sky;
see the enemy and truth in the green lane;
unafraid, unafraid, see sunlight and the planes.

(1943)

Peccavimus[7]

Now we are ashamed
of what we have been and have not been; the athlete
clear play of shoulderblades in the excellent back
bent to the oar and all for holiday
in lives of holiday; the dancer,
whine and scuffle on the polished floor
in the bright dive; the don
matching dead Roman against dead Carthaginian.

And all for nothing;
the stile in the gap of fence.
The easy stepping and the empty road
through life to death

and what we have not been
have not the words for; how declare

---

7. The title means "we have sinned." First published under the pseudonym Haydon Weir in *War Poems of the United Nations*, 50-51.

225

the double brotherhood of the Underground
where working chaps ride home, or sleep, or struggle,
in our boneless precision of language? How say
the weight on your shoulder of a piece of work
or an enemy's hand; we who toiled not
neither did we fight until now; but always of course
forgave our enemies.

And now we are ashamed;
would be serviceable, reclaim our value,
justify the lions in our scutcheon[8]
with some piece of heraldic valour against the night
the long dive in annihilation with the bombs
leaving the future to the men who earned it.

(1943)

Belated Discovery

But we were told before that we were at war;
told so often we could not hear it any more.

We had been told by the starved kitten in the alley
sharp haunches cowering from human feet
when cruelty was walking in the street.
We had been told by the child who played in the alley
with flaws of rickets in her fingerbones;
we had been told by the women in the alley
picking dinner out of garbagecans.

We had not heard.
It was too quiet and too subtle a word.
We needed to be told by the starved child,
by the woman lying with her hair spilled

8. A shield.

in a fan of dirty blood; by a loud noise
and a falling house;

                    not by the fall of tears.
They were too quiet for our simple ears.

                                      (December 1943)

The Dead Partisan[9]

When the sun laughed his first laugh
across the bright world,
at the time for shooting people
they brought out the man.

The man they were shooting
came walking out singing
with a smile on his mouth
and his face to the sun;
he kissed with his lips
the clean air of daybreak;

then they stood him
against a clean wall.

Then, in the moment between the trigger and the gun,
in the moment between the gun and the bullet,
in the moment between the decent air of morning
and the dead hands clutching the bloody grass,
the dead man spoke to us with his live eyes.

He said: fear nothing but fear.
Fear the rat at your heart
sick on poisoned bread;

9. First published in *Seven Poets in Search of an Answer*, ed. Thomas Yoseloff (New York: Bernard Ackerman, 1944), 30-31.

fear the snake in your belly
rubbing along the ground;
fear the worm in your head
crawling without a sound;

he said: be afraid
of no bullet, of no pain.

This man who was dead
looked at us and said:
only be afraid
not to be men.

(1943 or 1944)

Dialogue for D-Day[10]

My child born in the red year opens his fingers
and what have I got to put inside his hand?

Give him a toy, give him the world to jingle
as it will be when he is a man.

The world is too small for this small hand;
it is a shrunk and withered apple
rotten with death at the heart.

It is an apple with the seeds of life
golden at its heart.

The world will bite too hard for this small hand;
its teeth are sharp and poisonous with lies.
It is a skull with swastikas for eyes.

---

10. First published in *New Masses* 51 (June 20, 1944): 15.

It is the brainpan of a living man
singing with the future. It will speak
in promises of honey summertime;
Give it to your child.

How do I know
the world is safe for little hands to hold?
He is not one year old.

We go
across the hungry sea to make it so.

(1943 or 1944)

Poem for Liberation[11]

In the valley of briars northward from Barcelona
the ivory bones of Roland and his horn
make nibbles for the mice. Deep, deep
all those who fought the Moors. Only
the piping wind sings battle.
                                And the thorn
impales our empty and forgotten bones
lying in their last innocence asleep.

                        Here
the world came to an end. Here in the lonely

---

11. In this poem Davidman recalls an important incident from *La Chanson de Roland*, the well-known French poem that celebrates the Battle of Roncesvalles in 778. At the end of *Chanson*, Roland, headstrong but brave, whose forces are surrounded by their enemies, foolishly rejects advice to blow his horn in order to summon assistance from Charlemagne. The hopeless battle commences and Roland decides too late to blow his horn. Davidman shifts the setting of her poem forward to the French and Spanish countrysides of World War II and attempts to invoke the spirit of courage and bravery of Roland for the modern-day fighters defending their countries. First published in *New Masses* 52 (September 12, 1944): 8.

valley we left our courage and our hearts
and Durandal[12] broken on the stones.

The sword is broken but the horn unbroken....

                       And the horn lies
hollow in the hollow grass, and the wind cries,
and Comrade Roland has roots inside his eyes.

In the valley of thorns, up north from Catalonia,
we set down the burden of our bodies
and left our courage broken on the stones....

                Only the horn unbroken
singing in the singing grass
                   midway between France and Spain

The battle talk is spoken underground
by the wise moles, but only in whispers;
what then can come of this?

climbs in the whispering sap, sharpens the thorn:
but the dead lie still.

The dead lie still, but something is not still;
The battle talk is whispered to the horn
by the chittering mouse, by the wind's rising roar,
by the seething bush, by the great shout of trees,
and thunder, thunder, over the Pyrenees....
                Comrade Roland,
Cumpaing Rollanz, car sunez vostre cor![13]

                         (July 9, 1944)

12. Roland's sword.

13. Davidman's note to the poem: "(Last line is from the *Chanson de Roland*, the national epic of France. 'Comrade Roland, sound your horn now.')"

That Time Five Years Ago

That time five years ago I climbed your hill
And saw you walk between the light and me,
I went away and wrote the memory
Into some fourteen lines. And still, and still,
A bitter fragrance rises from that sonnet;
It was not wise, it was not great, alas!
And Shakespeare might have laughed; and yet it has
The mark of madness and of love upon it.

And I am not as mad as I was then;
Time brings a sad sobriety, I fear,
And I'm a wife and mother all this year
And do not vex my soul for stranger men
Than the sufficient one I'm married to;
The prose I have, the poems went with you.

(*August 4, 1944*)

How about It?

And they came back and it was all as before;
the dry leaves talking softly in the home street
and the light being gentle with the houses,
kiss of autumn, a light softer than a girl.
The leaves died under their feet.

They came back
to the white houses or the easy apartments;
open the burner and the gas stove lights,
press a button and the icebox sings;
back to the huckleberry pie as advertised
and the smooth electric razor, and the bed,
scented with Cobra, Dangerous, My Sin,
and it was all as before.

231

The bright replenished red paint shone on the gas pumps.
The car glittering highway was decently dressed in billboards.
The smokesweet darkness hung in the movie houses
with the lips on the screen, with the knee in the next chair,
and it was all very lovely as before.

And Abraham L. Lee found everything just as it had been
up the broken stair, past the sagging door, inside the four walls
where the mice ate the roaches and the rats ate the mice;
and he found he still had the same job, wasn't that nice,
for there's one thing we'll always need and that's a handyman,
and if he didn't feel grateful when he came back,
why, it just goes to show you, for Abraham Lee was black.

(1944)

Sonnet to Various Republicans[14]

The frightened man, over the abyss of time,
sees the tiny fields of future lie
bright as a landscape in an opal's eye,
a hundred years below, too far to climb
down, too far to crawl down, too far to get down by
undulating meekly like a worm
to the lovely watermeadows and the corn;
the only way to get there is to fly.

Denies the angel at his shoulderblade
prickling the skin of his poor back with wings;
retains the ape who tumbled through the air
and did not die, and cowers in the blood
afraid to fall. Cries, "There is nothing there,
Nothing but ruin and the death of kings."

(1944)

14. First published in *New Masses* 53 (December 19, 1944): 10.

In Memory of Herman Bottcher[15]

I knew a man once and he was a fool.
He might have stayed at home;

sat in the tulip garden, drinking his beer;
sat at the family table, eating his veal;
had a tulip wife, pink, white, and yellow.

But was a fool;
had no tact, no true humility,
no ... what's the word, stay-at-homes and gentlemen?
Something to express a weakness in the hams
that kept you sitting in the family garden
while Hitler roared above the tulips?

No?

You have the word but not the heart to say it?
O but you had the heart and the comfortable seat
and the common sense, you called it, while your neighbor
went his fool's way to the concentration camp.

(A man did pretty well
in the sanitary paradise of the superstate
if he had tact, adaptability,
an infinitely shut and smiling mouth,
in the hams a weakness, in the heart a fear,
and a voluntary blindness in the eye.)

And who's to say you were wrong to be afraid?
We are not to reproach you, we did a good business
with the pieces of our L train, with our oil

15. Herman John Bottcher (1909-1944) was an American soldier born in Germany, who was awarded the rank of captain in two different armies, the International Brigade during the Spanish Civil War and the United States Army during World War II. He saw extensive action in the Pacific during World War II and was killed during the Battle of Leyte in the Philippines on December 31, 1944.

and a certain kiss of death called nonintervention.
We were not remarkable for the erect position
said to be characteristic of the human race,
the way you tell it from the ape and swine.

Only he
might cast the first stone,[16] since he was a fool.
Took his turn in the concentration camp
learning to bend his knees, or so you'd think,
but needed more teaching, so he went to Spain.
A man that borrows trouble is a fool.

(The way with trouble,
why, you sit home, you don't go out to find it,
and nobody is going to dump it in your lap.
We're doing pretty well in Germany;
of course, there's the SS and the Gestapo,
and this, and that, and the ... well, my friend, I know
when to stop talking. And there's my three boys
dead somewhere in the East; and the house and garden
the way you see them; dig down fifteen feet,
you'll find the dinner table and Hildegarde,
just as she was dishing up the first roast we'd had in weeks.
But after we win the war, things will be fine.
I'll get me an American girl with the nice long legs;
a man gets lonely without Hildegarde.)

All this the fool rejected, and for what?
The wind of Spain that eats a man's lungs out,
the food of Spain that never was enough
to kill the bitter taste, the taste of defeat.
And then America wouldn't have him back.
Premature and excessive was the word.

16. Davidman alludes here to the biblical story of the woman caught in adultery:
"So when they continued asking [Jesus], he lifted up himself, and said unto them, He
that is without sin among you, let him first cast a stone at her" (John 8:7).

You fool, if you must be so arrogant,
to stand erect when the world goes on all fours,
you'll find teeth meeting in the calf of your leg,
you, premature hero, premature man.

They let him in at last,
and out again by the golden western door
to the fabulous murderous islands where the palms
are tattered with bullets. And Leyte got him;
he lies with the bright ribbons of valor
between his heart and the worms. Over his head
the island whispers love, love and remembrance.

Might have stayed at home
and died comfortably the rat's death
in comfortable Germany, but was a fool.

(1944)

Tourist Folder

Aren't you tired
and wanting change;
do you want a good time
do you want a good time?

The job gives you the pip;
life gives you the pip;
aren't you tired;
wouldn't you like a change?

Why
pack up your troubles in your new pigskin valise
come where Broadway lies festering with light
lies dreaming.

Leave the small house at the edge of the small town at the
edge of enormous unpopulated night;
come where New York lies gleaming.

You never saw a city like this one;
never was a city like this one,
up in the air like arrows to the sun,
burning a hole in the sky. You never saw
windows gleam as a million windows gleam.
You never had such a marvelous dream.

Come see New York;
the women walk
hips twinkling up Fifth Avenue,
lovely, lovely, lovely, none for you;
the air tastes different there
breathed by a billionaire;

the city flows like silk in your throat;
they never turn off the electric lights.
You never get tired of the yellow night
and the special sunlight on the fur coats,
and the taxicabs in a rainbow stream.
You never had such a miraculous dream.

But there's something you haven't seen just yet;
you've got another thrill to get.
Come ride in the subway from here to the Bronx
with the cheap people, the valueless ones,
the ten cent store women, the drafted men,
the faces bitter and chewed by pain,
the creatures crawling home from work
who stand, who wait, who also serve.[17]

17. This is an ironic allusion to lines from John Milton's sonnet "When I Consider
How My Light Is Spent":

> "God doth not need
> Either man's work or his own gifts; who best

Brother, now you see New York
when it gets rough
and elbows your eye.

And observe: we starve.
And overhear: we cough.
And deduce: we die.

Have you had a good time?

(1944?)

Goodbye, the Soldier Said

Never's a long time not to see your face
Whether you hide it in the dirty ground
Or in ten thousand miles of distances;
Never's a long time not to hear the sound
Of your memorable and remembered voice
Saying words you both are thinking of;
Never couple, never quarrel, never kiss,
Never's a long time not to have your love.

Also always is a very long time,
And your mouth, your eyelids, and your smile
May hit sea bottom in a little while;
Soldier, don't turn over in the slime
When her bridegroom walks into her chamber;
Always is a long time to remember.

(1944?)

Bear his mild yoke, they serve him best. His state
Is Kingly. Thousands at his bidding speed
And post o'er Land and Ocean without rest:
They also serve who only stand and wait."

Tin Pan Alley

What else is there but wind and rain
for girls to tangle in their hair
at crying time, what else is there
but the word pain to speak of pain?

Nightly the repeated moon
overhears her loud despair;
but she has said it all before,
like the dog that bays the moon.

She has said it all before,
she will say it all again,
every time the young men
pass by her front door.

(1944?)

Midwinter Song

As I have heard
talkers tell,
four angry rivers
run around hell.

The river death,[18]
it hurts the most,
yet in a breath
it can be crossed;

the river fire[19]
will serve your turn,

18. In Greek mythology this was the river Styx.
19. The river Phlegethon.

till you have no heart
left to burn.

The one called pain[20]
is a salty river;
it pickles your brain
forever and ever.

In a million years,
or more, or less,
you'll reach the river
forgetfulness.[21]

(1944?)

When You Got the Row of Holes

When you got the row of holes
stitched in your chest, you were alone
with a pair of wings.
                    The plane
turned birdwise, slipped
sidewise out of the sky.
                    And you, soldier,
you were afraid to die
so much alone.

But I was there too when you died;
I saw your eyes roll up;
I saw your eyes turn white.

(1944?)

20. The river Acheron.
21. The river Lethe.

Quisling at Twilight[22]

Houses are quiet at evening. The sad colors
are sliding down the cypresses. Quiet, quiet.
Eyes look out of the sky, and the roof hides you
but the house is quiet.
                          So many empty chairs,
so many handsome rooms and no one in them
but the company of lights.

Turn on all the lights. Sit in the armchair,
not the one facing the mirror but the one
next to the friendly fire but no not there
where the fire makes pictures out of memory; there
next to the window but no not that the glimmering pane
shows you your eyes; here here by the desk
but you see your face in the polish of the desk.

So much fine furniture but it costs too much
at evening with the sad colors and the voices
you know it costs too much.

The beetle ticks in the walls.
The woman beaten till the child in her womb
leaped once and was dead, is sobbing in the garden
under the parrot perches.

The broken fingers
of the twelve-year-old boy scuttles across the floor
or was it rats again.
                          So many rats
and someone here to feed them.

---

22. This poem focuses upon the interior life of a quisling — the World War II term
used by Allies for one who collaborated with the enemy. First published in *New Masses*
56 (July 31, 1945): 4. This was Davidman's last poem to appear in *New Masses*.

(but you meant no harm did you and there was nothing
else you could do was there and they promised order
a new order and you thought they would win
and there was a standard of living to maintain and a blonde
and you were afraid

and somebody had to keep the mob in its place
and you were afraid

and after all you were never the one who did the killing)

The desk and the mirror and the windowpane.
Nowhere to go where you cannot see your face.

The dead hands fumble for the latch.

(1945)

Tragic Muse[23]

Poor poet,
they have killed you too often. The bird does not sing.
They have buried you too often with the jagged bones of children
sprouting from the hasty trench. They have burned you in locked
    churches.
They have shut you in with the secret sigh of gas
too often, too often, too often, too often, too often.
You hung on meathooks in the Romanian slaughterhouse.

And so the bird does not fly any more. Brass parrots
scream to the gilt-edged trees. Clockwork
sits in the birdcage and trills like a canary.
Death burns the heart.

23. This poem alludes to the Battle of Teruel, which was fought in the harsh winter
of 1937-1938 in and around the city of Teruel — a city in Aragon, eastern Spain — during
the Spanish Civil War. After a series of bloody battles, the Nationalists eventually
wrested control of the city from the Republicans.

The heart burns the breast.
Nightlong you hung in the Romanian slaughterhouse
thinking of the end of time and the flyhusk world
sucked out by spiders. Obscene laughter
shattered the dark with flares. The world ended.
The meathook burned in your heart.

After these nights
what song to morning, what gladness arising
dewdabbled, sweet, to the sun on the elms? O trees
stooping merciful, hide the unsinging bird;
the cold dew dripping from the leaves
makes pain unremembering. Forgetfulness
falls from the leaves, sleep, sleep falls from the leaves
and the long willowhair blinds the staring eyes
under the branches. Do not ask her to sing any more.
She is tired.

O wind
cold over the Atlantic, sealifter
cloudshaker wind from the Spanish rock, bear witness:
the voice cried, the earth moved, the trees danced.
Who would not sing for Spain?

But that was on the hill over Teruel
when the jewel hung poised between the worlds
and death waited and the schools were still open
and the dreamers marching; and the child
broken to pieces in the play street
was an unexpected thing to see in the paper.

Those days we wept easily, the throat filled
and blew big bubbles of words. The first time we died
it was an unexpected thing, and we talked about it.
We guessed the worms in our halfeaten eyes
angels of speedy resurrection. And then Franco

and the career diplomat, the obscene bird.
The river and the darkness and the jaws.

The clockwork bird has glass gold eyes
and feathers painted pretty as lies;
you wind it up with a key, click click;
and a song comes out of its mouth, clack clack.
O the bird singing, the poor pretty polly, full of mechanical starfire
and its cage is golden and its claws are golden
and above all the key, the key is golden;
you put the key in its heart, click click,
and a poem comes out of its mouth, clack clack.

Harsh throat, be silent.
Hang on your hook and beat the bloodied air
with foolish wings. It does not matter;
the sky will not fall, and the moon and stars will not
be squeezed screaming from their places. This is only human death,
the soldier whom it took twenty years to make
smashed willfully in a moment, the dead baby,
breathed once and the air burned him. Shed your tears,
plant the sterile headstone over the grave
and make new children. Not in your time
perhaps, the whiteness, the singing and the peace,
and men will die whatever you can do;
but there is always the miracle, the child.

(1945)

This Year of the Atom

This is it;
this is the sunless moment the black hole
deep in space where no stars set foot
and the earth goes voyaging and gets lost.
This is the cavern in the belly of time
rattling with darkness.

                         Here the babies lie
of the rotten womb of now; corrupt, and die.
Who chokes us at birth? blows our light out?
breaks the mirror of our eyes across
and kicks us out of the back door of life?
Who says no to us?
                         Who but ourselves
lovesick for fingers that are let lie quiet
being fleshless; weeping with love
for lying still in the hidey-hole of ground
six feet deep, a paradise of sleep,
while the world rolls its hoop.

Sun come up;
revive, bloody and immaculate courage
of the live body. Reestablish us;
ordain, hearten, and reanimate us.
Let this wriggler, this progressor on his belly
extend the impossible joints of his legs and get up.
Remember it was done before, out of the slime.

We are stuck in the spiderweb of time,
juiceless, hung between this hour and the next,
while the jaws go suck suck.

Well well;
who's afraid of spiders?

Sun come up;
let the web shrivel and the suspended men
walk on their legs across the living world.

This is it, this is nadir, the moment
wet and black at the bottom of the world
before the rotation lifts the ocean over the horizon
bright, painted with brightness, wearing
light, heartbreaking light.

The light is quiet.
The dry bones lift themselves out of the bottomless ditch,
assemble into man and go to get their breakfast.

Sun, rise and shine.

(1945?)

Next Step

As I came up the dialectical spiral time
took me by the throat and forced me into incarnation
in the body of his death. No longer
immortal in the blind swirl of the atom,
immortal in the blind careening of the star.
No longer existing yesterday and tomorrow
but pinned to now with the dagger of this death.

No longer perdurable[24]
in the rock, in the waterdrop, in the crystal
with pure violet spears dissecting the day's eye; no longer
innocent, the rose. No longer
unknowing, the cameleopard[25] in the spotted land,
chameleon in the changeable desert, flittermouse,
bird in the belly of the wind.

Death
lies not in death, but in the knowing it.
I have borne the incarnation. I have faced the mirror:
not to be star any longer but earth; not
rock any longer but flesh; not
cold rose but breathing bird.

24. Eternal or everlasting.
25. "Cameleopard" is the archaic word for a giraffe.

Not unknowing,
not innocent, safe, immortal any longer.
Not to be ape any longer but man.

In the hour of our death,
in the hour of our knowing of our death.

As I came up the dialectical spiral time
rose and laughed at me. Here
is the topmost step in the spiral staircase
and here the fall from the burning tower. Here
is as high as you will go.

High enough,
just high enough to see how far you will fall,
the height you will fall from, down the dizzying air.

Death
is not in striking the ground, but in falling,
the moment of falling, the eternity of falling;
or in your first look down from the top of the tower.

Time stared and grinned. And I,
not being ape any longer but man,
bore the incarnation and fronted the stare
and found the next step with my certain foot,
the invisible step ascending the dizzy air.

(1946)

Mushroom Gathering

The child who walked in the twittering wood
Went that way for love of the trees;
Nothing in life was quite as good
As pluming her nose with the maple keys.[26]

There was no profit under the leaves
Except the golden leaf in her hand,
Only the joy that moves and breathes
And does not trouble to understand,

And that is not enough for her now.
She has shrewder and narrower eyes,
And she looks for pleasures that grow
Out of the ground, not out of the skies,

Mushrooms, good when you get them home
And when dried almost equally good,
Reason enough for a woman to come,
Reason enough to walk in the wood;

Yet she will lift her eyes from profit
At times, and stare at the maple keys
Or a lonely poplar with sun upon it,
Singing and gold as a hive of bees.

(1946?)

March 21st

Went walking just now in the naked time,
pause between sleep and waking of the year,
with nothing positive to set the heart on,

26. The fruit of the maple tree, often called a whirlybird.

no red leaf, blue shadow. O abomination;
clear sharp immitigable winter gone
and nothing in its place.

Now mourn for winter;
oh all the bright winds and the arrowy sunflakes
departed, ah the lovely cruelty,
the hanging ice in spears above our heads
departed; mourn.

Here now
lie last year's crumpled papers in the gutter
and mud and dogturds; and the sky is doubtful.

Went walking in this wilderness of bones,
treebones confounded of the dead and living
naked alike; bones of the broken reeds
and grey unhappy cornstalks, and the rat
some dog chewed last November, disinterred
exposing his minim architecture of ribs.

O boneyard time, stripped to the naked nothing,
ugly and expectant, the pause before the flowers.

(1947)

After Hiroshima[27]

Let us have no more leaves.
The lilacs are a lie,
The silver sun deceives.
Let us have no more sky.

27. This poem alludes to the dropping of the atomic bomb on the Japanese city of
Hiroshima on August 6, 1945.

See, under grassy ground
These are the things that are;
The earth a burning wound,
The sea a naked scar;

At the bleached bone of it
Stares the blind moon;
We have not done this yet,
But we will do it soon.

(1947?)

When They Grow Up

I bore my sons before the bomb
Burned up so many Japanese
And ashes that were babies blew
Among the bamboo trees.

It was not new to kill a child;
A new invention, though,
To do it quite so perfectly,
So many at one blow.

I have two sons, two sons, two sons,
And terror in my head;
Small feet play safely on the lawn,
Small hearts beat safe in bed,

Bird voices, fragile birdlike bones,
Small hands that grasp my hands;
I bore my sons before the bomb.
Once I made plans.

(1947?)

The Haunted Atheist[28]

O in what low lights wandering your face
came to me first out of the swamp laughter
and the all together snicker of the reeds in damp places;

after the knife-thrust and the last gurgle, after
the crucified arms beating the sky like flails
and the night coming soft but the death coming softer;

how wandering through what multitudinous hells,
that of the moth beating blind eyes; of the silence
with the moon shut out; of the sour screaming seagulls;

hell of the slow beetles at the bottom of the trench;
hell of the sharp seat upon the barbed wire;
of the gas bubbles forming in the veins

as we came up from under seas where
the fire-eyed fishes chewed us, with the drowned
men tangling their hair in our long hair;

and in every cloud in every sound
and color and thunder of dawn; silver
of moonrise; leer upon the ground

of the slick snake; pointed finger
of poplar tree; windshape and watershape,
ghost in the sunlight, bird beneath the river,

spotted fishskin, drumming chest of ape,
all beasts and all claws and all kisses.
No escape, no escape, and no escape

28. Although we cannot date Davidman's conversion precisely, this poem marks the beginning of several that deal explicitly with her movement toward Christianity. For more on her conversion, see her autobiographical essay, "The Longest Way Round," *Bone*, 83-97.

from your remembered face in wildernesses;
no hiding place in rock, no hole in sand;
no paradise behind the watercresses

in a place that is neither water nor land,
the little cavern at the waterfall's foot;
your suffering lips and brows on every hand.

O you the laughter, you the pursuit
and the vain dream; ghost, bird, and Son of Man.
I built a happiness to shut you out.

Hell would not keep you out, nor earth. I ran
to see what heaven could do. In vain, my dear;
your questionable shape comes even here.

(1947?)

Assumption

I had a daunting dream the other night.
Eternity, that ring of endless light
Vaughan-dubbed,[29] I saw, and thought
"It's very vague! 'll
Be made clearer, do you think, by Hegel?"[30]

For I'd been reading books profound and deep
Before I wearily dropped off to sleep.
I saw a band of toilers reach the height
Where everything at last was calm and bright.

And then a Presence that I thought I saw
Filled me with sudden overpowering awe.

29. Henry Vaughan (1621-1695) was a physician and metaphysical poet greatly influenced by hermetic philosophy.

30. Georg Wilhelm Friedrich Hegel (1770-1831) was a German philosopher; one of his most influential ideas was speculative logic or "dialectic."

But all the band began to set up chairs
And stand on them — to lead in hymns or prayers?

Not so! To state the strict determinism
That lifted them at last from the abysm
Of Earth below. It seemed there was no doubt
That all along they knew it would work out

Exactly as it had. I could not follow
Their arguments resounding high and hollow.
I felt the Holy Ghost a living presence.
But what in — time — is dialectic essence?

(1947?)

Lines for a Lazy Husband

Bees in the honeysuckle,
Bees in the clover,
Singing the same tune
Over and over.

Tune about summer,
Tune about honey;
Winter will find us
Without any money,

No coal in the cellar
And we're sure to freeze;
But we've smelled the clover
And we've heard the bees.

Wasps in the windows,
Ants in the beds;
The old roof is falling
Down on our heads;

We had a lawn once
A baby could lie on;
We've lost it since
To the dandelion;

Squeak! the door goes,
Ding-dong! the bell;
Pigs in the parlor
And puss in the well;

Oodles of money
We owe Uncle Sam,
But we've lived on honey
And wild-strawberry jam.

(1948?)

The Foolish Virgin[31]

My lamp was full of holy light;
It should have lasted all the night.

As I was hastening on the road
I heard a child cry in the wood;

The night was dark, the wood was wild;
I turned aside and found the child,

I found a child who else had died;
There was a great hole in his side,

And the lamp's glimmer showed me how
Nails pierced his feet and thorns his brow.

---

31. The title of this poem alludes to the parable of the ten wise and foolish virgins in Matthew 25:1-13.

I quenched the flame against the ground,
I used the oil to salve his wound,

I took him home, I gave him bread,
Lulled him to sleep in my own bed.

I'm late, I know it is a sin;
Lord, may I not enter in?

(1948?)

Love, in the Lonely Night

Love, in the lonely night
with small rain falling,
do not you lie awake
to hear me calling.

Love, in your still chamber,
however loudly
knocks my heart's hammer,
love, sleep soundly.

Be not disquieted.
I ring no bell
to wake you for my need;
love, sleep well.

Christ, in the lonely night
grant me a prayer;
him, not to know;
me, not to care.

(1948?)

Chimney Corner

You would not think it now, but we were young
one time, went wandering in the sweet white clover
and watched the bees make honey. That was all
we needed then for love, a clover field
and honey and the sun; when we were young.

The honey is eaten from the comb.
The bees are dead, the clover is cut down.

They planted wheat where clover once had grown,
and then we were not old. You would not think it,
one harvest-time we kissed among the sheaves;
sweet, sweet, the crickets and the harvest moon
enormous gold, a moon you could get drunk on,
laugh, lie back on the strawstack with your throat
gleaming under the moon, and take his love.
The moon was all we had, we lived on moon.

And time went on, the night wore out to dawn,
the wheat was eaten and the moon went down.

Now in the comfortable house that keeps the wind
from quenching fires and rattling these old bones
I tell my memories over like my beads
and see you smiling at them. Is it strange
that flesh can perish like the wheat and clover,
that love is eaten, like the bread and honey?
We are all tidbits for the tooth of time
to mumble over. See how it has gnawed
the trace of kisses from this lip and throat;
there is no sign of any kiss but time's.

Pleasant it was to lie down in the clover.
Sweet it was, embracing in the wheat.
Sweet, sweet, to warm old bones, remembering
in the chimney corner, in the peaceful house.

Why then
must sorrow come and clank his iron chain
between the past and present? It was good,
time that it was; good now, remembering
that it has been. Past, past;
why should the word fall on our ears like death?

If we knew that
we should know why we are born and why we die.
And I am very old and much at peace
and have but little sorrow when I say it:
I loved him once, and it was long ago.

And yet
there should be somewhere I shall find again
the wheat, the clover, honey, sun, and love.

(September 1949)

The Safe People

Desert we crossed, the first time coming barefoot,
firewalk between the cactus and the snake;
by day the cruel colors, and a night
of skullbright stars. Walked till the heart broke.
Some lived, and many died, and all were saved.

Desert we crossed, second time in the wagons,
childbirth over the groaning axletree
on the spread floursacks; the Indian guns;
the cattle died of thirst and so did we;
we left our skin and bones and we got on.

Crossed then with locomotives on our backs.
Our feet were hammers driving in the spikes;
the rails flowed after and filled in our tracks.

Died in our sweat, died shouting in our sins,
lived sometimes to grow rich, yet most were saved.

                      The last time
crossed in the smooth sealed trains and in the planes,
sucked at our vices, hardly knew we crossed,
safe in our envelope of precooled air.
Now there are no more deserts anywhere
but the burning territory in our brains
where the lone figure crumples. We are lost.

                                        (1949)

Selva Oscura[32]

I
In my bitterness and my rattling pride
I turned my back upon my lord and lover
and walked away with nothing at my side
but a lean dog called death. For fear of laughter

and being left alone, I walked alone,
pleased with the dog's breath hot upon my hand.
I said: this is the way to warm my bones.

And this is wisdom in a weary land;
ask nothing, shut your teeth upon your need;
give nothing, shut your heart against his words
whose eyes would melt your armor off and lead
you naked through a world of sprouting swords;

---

32. *Selva oscura*, the dark wood or forest, alludes to the opening lines of Canto I of Dante's *Inferno*: "Midway this way of life we're bound upon, I woke to find myself in a dark wood, / Where the right road was wholly lost and gone" (ll. 1-3; *The Comedy of Dante Alighieri: Hell*, trans. Dorothy L. Sayers [Harmondsworth, Middlesex, UK: Penguin, 1949]). Metaphorically, *selva oscura* suggests that at this point in Davidman's life she may have been disoriented — politically, morally, spiritually, physically, and intellectually.

who never asks can never be denied;
you have your pride and you shall keep your pride.

II
O but the Dog came padding after me
breath hot upon my hand, till I began
somewhat to weary of my company;
I turned and saw his teeth, and then I ran

through lust and terror and tormented nights;
through the sword-groves and the poisonous air,
while the moon filled my mind with barren light.

Someone caught me by the snaky hair
and laughed: I am your safety, linger here.
I said: But I must run, I am pursued
by what was once my chosen follower.
Here is no safety but in spilling blood;

The Dog is hungry and he must be fed.
Let him eat you instead of me, I said.

III
Who came between us in the dismal wood,
between the Dog and me? I saw him fall
and heard out of the darkness and the blood
the steel teeth worrying his heart. Kind fool,

poor loving fool, I said, such end has love.
At least your death has bought me time to run.
I will be wise and cower in a cave.

At the wood's edge, against the rising sun,
the dead fool risen came to me again
and a tame dog went leaping harmlessly
before his shining feet. I knew him then,
my love and friend. The world shall end, I said,

before I can forgive myself. And he:
But I forgave before the world was made.

(February 1951)

Doubting Castle[33]

I
Neither belief nor knowledge; not the spring
with innumerable grasshopper voices
reborn in the old song; nor yet the winter
frozen in certainties; not one of these
but the naked ugliness of March,
time between seasons, and the restless trees
and aching mud, and wind that prophesies

of what, to what, among the dead men; none
to answer in the field of broken bones.
Give us our hearts, give us our breath, O God
and stand us up on our brave feet; for we
lie here dead and unburied till we stale
the unsprouting cornfield with our poisonous bones.

Who now could cry for rain, who for rebirth
rattle the ashes of this peace? Arrested
at the edge of death, dried out and laid aside;
blood of returning life would hurt us worse
than any more destruction. Bury us
or stand us up on brittle feet, O God;
men should live or be dead, but not between.

---

33. The title of this poem alludes to the episode in John Bunyan's allegory *The Pilgrim's Progress* (1678) when Christian is captured by the Giant Despair and thrown into Doubting Castle.

II
Why but a skeleton's a pretty thing
in the springtime, the pretty ring time,
all neatly dead and finished, absolute,
strict and naked, ultimate as ice.
And a live man with the skin on him
pretty to see, goes shining in the sun,
pink gauze and iridescent wing and eyes,
grasshopper voices million in the night.
One should be live or dead.
                              But not like this,
the crawling corpse, the eyelids moved by maggots,
the deathwatch beetle ticking in the heart
and the electric wires to move our hands
in the sterile laboratory where a corpse
operates on corpses to make them rise.
They have buried us but not quite deep enough,
the prophet wind rattles our jaws together,
plays tongue between our teeth.
                              How dead are we
when we cannot even tell if we are dead?
Chained up in the undertaker's castle,
disguised in neon, sleeked in television,
the fatface senator floating belly up
corpsemouthed in corruption; the sages
discreet in newsprint; the future
so pissed upon, so bemerded, beworded
it is as stale as the past.
                              Lord, lord,
out of the cellar of the giant's castle
deliver us, that we may live or die.

III
All shapes are no shape; all colors
a shaken intensity of rainbow nothings
on a gray nothing; all loves
a scrabble of dry fingers on the stones.

O we have seen too much and cannot see,
have heard and jangled all the songs to deafness,
have married all the angels to the devils
in marriage as sterile as a mule; no child
of these is born in light, no son of man,
but corpses breeding corpses in the dust.
Mummyskin, the hollow chest splits open,
full of dry beetles clicking their dry words.

Yet it was not
God whom we doubted, but it was ourselves
we did not think existed; where's man?
Not in the thrills and prickles of his body.
Inside his head? Why not smash up the head
and try to find him in it?
                              And we could not
find him; the sight was real but not the seer,
yes the beloved flesh was a real thing
but not the love and therefore not the lover;
we spaded clods upon our newmade grave
and danced a dance of dry skin and dead bones
to tread them down.
                              Yet when love
wakes the returning waters, and the wind
strangles the naked trees, we are aware,
O Love, that we are not buried deep enough;
we might stand up, if you should call with love.

IV
They make their castles out of air these days;
neither shapes nor colors; no walls
but the curved wind of space. Bone-prison,
space-prison, nutshell, never-get-out-cell
with something locked inside it screaming; skull.
Windows to look on everduring dark.

Neither clouds nor colors. Let us out.

O you almighty storms that wreck the mountains
you cannot shake this prison; O you blasts
of manfire ruining cities, mushroom clouds
grown in a morning's pride, you cannot make
the least small ripple in the windy curve
of space that walls the soul in. Let me go,
follow the labyrinthine music, flow
out of closed space and time to that which lies
past all dimensions and their mysteries,
timeless, starless, neverdarkling, Is.

V

The pit is in my belly and I drum
on my own skin stretched tightly over it;
the stars are in my head and I become
a skin of space used to lock in the pit;
why this is hell nor am I out of it.

The fires are in my guts and you may light
a candle at them that will do no good;
it will not serve to lead you home at night,
it will not help to thaw your frozen blood;
sputter and dribble, put it out in mud.

Dust and a little spittle, such am I.
I am the vulture tearing my own heart.
I am the cupped hand that contains the sky
and the dark Nothing sitting down apart
from all made things; but if I am, Thou art.

(*March* 31, 1951)

Easter

In the pure spring, the pure awakening waters
lap at the willows' feet under our bridges
cold music, and the swallow twitters
in last year's rushes;

from the unchanging stone the water comes
live, cold, leaping, fishskin silver; morning
shines momentarily, then dims
with white rain falling.

No longer than by subtle and silver flashes,
no louder than the sprouting corn,
or a grey catbird's hints and hushes;
in these cold quiet ways we are reborn.

(April 7, 1951)

Prayer before Daybreak

I have loved some ghost or other all my years.
Dead men, their kisses and their fading eyes
dim in the house of memory; glimmers
in twilight air, no more. They were not there
to say no to me when I wanted them,
so it was safe to love them.
                                    And dead gods,
blind eyes in plaster in the safe museum,
the broken hands without the thunderbolt
and the lost mouths that could not laugh at prayers
I did not make to them.
                                    And a worse ghost,
the thin unearthly shadow of tomorrow
scudding ahead of my realities,
that since it never could be overtaken

could never disappoint me.

$\qquad\qquad\qquad$ Dear shadows,
images of bare branches on the snow
already melting; images
of dwindled sun in the shadows of eclipse
running like ghosts of snakes along the ground
while the moon's shadow passes. Ghosts of ghosts,
the twittering echoes of the strengthless dead
who do no harm.

Only the terrible Now
I dared not love. Not the word made flesh,
not the Incarnation bearing a sword
to strike me to the heart; not that which is,
but is not I. Not God,
or sun, or blood, or anything real
that when I spoke it could not say no to me.

For I have loved my own ghost all these years
till there is nothing to say yes to me;
till there is only vast and lightless nothing
and in the heart of it not even I.

O Love, let shadows flee;
O live sun, living God, incarnate sword
of edged reality, let me be hurt,
but let me be alive enough to die. $\qquad$ (April 9, 1951)

Sapphics[34]

Now the moon is set;
the Pleiades are gone;

34. Named after the ancient Greek female poet Sappho, the Sapphic stanza in mod-
ern poetry is generally four lines that utilize trochees (a metrical foot with one stressed
syllable followed by an unstressed one) and dactyls (a stressed syllable followed by
two unstressed ones).

it is the hour of midnight,
and I lie down alone.

Someone did not come;
she wrote it with her tears.
Since she lay down alone
it is two thousand years.

Two thousand years and more
have blown away, since she
leaped from the white Greek shore
into the dark Greek sea.

Drowned, drowned and gone
under the cliff. O never
the golden-sandalled dawn
shall wake her to her lover.

Nightly the evening star
calls home the wandering sheep.
The willow tree's long hair
lets fall sleep

on other weary ones.
She will not come to see.
What hurt Sappho once
is all dissolved in sea;

why remember one
who has been gone so long?
Yet I lie down alone
singing her song.

(1952)

For Davy Who Wants to Know about Astronomy

All I know is what I've been told;
The Moon is silver, the sun is gold.

Coinsilver, moonsilver, buy me a tear;
I lost all of mine in a bygone year.

Coingold, sungold, buy me a kiss;
Love is for sale to coins like this.

What can you buy with the sun and moon?
A golden cradle, a silver spoon.

The cradle will turn to a sailing boat,
The spoon be a rudder that steers as you float,

The tears are a sea to sail upon,
The kiss is the wind that drives you on;

Of my sunlit days and my moony nights,
My forgotten tears and my lost delights,

I'll make a magic to ferry you soon
East of the sun and west of the moon.

(1952?)

Poems to C. S. Lewis (1952-1955)

Ballade of Blistered Feet

Morning a sparkle of blue
And air that one breathed with a thrill;
The world tasted fragrant and new
When we climbed over Shotover hill.[1]
Swallows were merry and shrill;
They cavorted all over the sky,
And we had the whole day to kill,
Jack and Warnie and I.

We came to a pub that we knew,
Whose sign was a queen in a frill,
And somehow before we were through
We drank rather more than our fill;
It *was* a bit careless to spill
Half of the beer in my eye;
But we were too gay to sit still,
Jack and Warnie and I.

What started as delicate dew
Grew up into rain, dank and chill;
I got a small lake in my shoe,

1. Shotover Hill is behind the Kilns, Lewis's home in Headington, a village just outside Oxford.

And all down my spine ran a rill;
There we were, halfway to Brill,
On ground that was naked and high —
Wet enough to distill,
Jack and Warnie and I!

Envoy

Ducks, I got home slightly ill
And more than ready to die;
But we'll do it again, so we will,
Jack and Warnie and I![2]

(Fall 1952)

Bread-and-Butter Sestina[3]

When the four winds stand dreaming on a hill
And half the sky is drowsy with a cloud
That falls asleep in rain, when swallows fill
Air with an airy music, and aloud
Rooks cry their queer occasions; when, until
Frost humbles them, the trees are gold and proud;

---

2. This poem, and most of those following, was written during Davidman's first trip to Oxford and subsequent meetings with C. S. Lewis and his brother, Warren, in the fall of 1952. She alludes to the day that inspired this poem in her letter to Chad Walsh of January 25, 1953; see *Out of My Bone: Letters of Joy Davidman* (Grand Rapids: Eerdmans, 2009), 138-39 (hereafter *Bone*).

3. Davidman refers to writing this sestina in her unpublished letters to Bill Gresham of October 4, 1952 ("I'm trying to write Jack a bread-and-butter letter in the form of a sestina, he having forbidden me to send the ordinary kind. Boy, is *that* a dilly of a verse-form — look it up. Going quite well, though"; Davidman's emphasis) and October 15, 1952 ("I'll enclose my sestina, which seems to have knocked Jack for a loop — he being one of the few people who can tell how hard that sort of thing is.... Remember that in the sestina the exact order of the end words in each stanza is prescribed all the way through!"). For more on the sestina verse form, see the Appendix.

O then I shall remember, and be proud
Of that ten miles I went by field and hill
And hawthorn hedge so merrily, until
We laughed the rain out of the hovering cloud
And small birds in the sunlight sang aloud;
On that September day I had my fill

Of country pleasures. Though the shadows fill
My heart and mind hereafter, still the proud
Horn in the morning clamoring aloud
To answering hounds on that remembered hill
Glimmers as one delight without a cloud
That never can be darkened — not until

I shrug my bones off, surely not until
No more is left of me than men can fill
A hole in clay with. Lofty as a cloud
The soul floats free, they say; yet not so proud
It cannot linger on some autumn hill
For one last look at lovely earth. Allowed

To choose my own goodbye, I'll cry aloud
A farewell through your windows; for until
I get a glimpse of Heaven's highest hill,
There is no sight so beautiful to fill
My memory, as Thames meadows with the proud
Towers of Oxford shining on a cloud.

And there was once a voice within a cloud
I would not hear, although it called aloud
In Love's own words; since I was bred too proud
For all gods but my bitter self, until
You taught me wisdom. Gratitude might fill
With hymns of joy, for that, your house and hill,

Your quiet hill; except I would not cloud
Or fill your eyes and ears with any loud
Mere thanks — until I am no longer proud!   (*October 15, 1952*)

Apologetic Ballade by a White Witch

I didn't really mean any harm
The night I stealthily locked the door,
Then muttered a white and wintry charm
And traced a pentacle on the floor;
That volume of forgotten lore
Said devils would rise and freeze me stiff;
But who believes the sages of yore?
I wanted to see what would happen, if . . .

All night around my lonely farm
The wind kept up a desolate roar;
Pale sunrise showed, to my alarm,
Roads that were glassy, trees that were hoar
With hairy icicles, meadows frore[4]
(Rhyme stolen from Shelley), swamp and cliff
Lost in the snow like the lost Lenore;
But I wanted to see what would happen, if . . .

Oxford is cold (and I'm not warm);
The blizzards drive upon sea and shore;
So magic truly can raise a storm!
But how does one lay it, I implore?
Why didn't I look *that* up before
I ventured upon my harmless whiff
Of hell's own brimstone? What a bore!
Still, I wanted to see what would happen, if . . .

Prince, I'll never do it no more!
My interest was purely scientif-
Ic (as doctors say when they bathe in gore);
I just wanted to see what would happen, if . . .[5]

(Fall 1952?)

4. Frozen.
5. At the end of the poem Davidman appends "(for C.S.L.)."

Threat: When I Come Back to Headington

When I come back to Headington,
I'll leave no footsteps where I walk;
My jokes will all have dwindled down
To thin and unamusing talk
Held between shadows and the wind
That blows a ghost from tree to tree;
And dogs who want to bite will find
Nothing solid left of me —

Only a something that can weep
And wring transparent hands, and plead
With one who lies too sound asleep
And, if he waked, would still not heed.
When I come back to Headington
I shall be dead as last year's hat
And stripped clean of my flesh and bone —
I shall not love you less for that.

(February 10, 1953)

Acrostic in Hendecasyllabics[6]

Could you listen to your devoted lover?
Listen just a while, it will soon be over —
In a day or two I shall lie contented,
Very straight and still, dead and unlamented.
Every word I said you will have forgotten,
Soon as I'm away and my bones are rotten.
Till then, listen then! Here's a little poem
After him who wrote — surely you must know him —

---

6. This poem is influenced by Catullus. The hendecasyllabic lines (lines of eleven syllables) were favored by the Latin poet, and the phrase *passer, deliciae* (sparrow, darling) alludes to one of his lyrics.

"*Passer, deliciae*" — what could be sweeter?
(Let me stop and see if I've got the meter.
End-rhymes thereunto, just to make it meaner;
Some day this whole page goes unto the cleaner,)
Look, my dearest, Jack, this is getting silly;
Each fool writes like this, even my poor Billy.
When I go to sleep, I'll make no more verses.
I feel gloomier than an empty hearse is;
So, sire, nighty-night. This is awful. Curses!

(February 14, 1953)

Valentine

Can you forgive me for the tacit lie —
Love concealed in friendship and in laughter?
I have played all my tricks upon you, I
Vainly ran to bring you running after;
Every woman knows the art, my lad!

Silly I was to try it, all the same;
Tomorrow, possibly, I may be glad
And grateful that one man saw through the game.
Perhaps, though, you'll remember when it's over
Lightly I did not tempt you; I was caught
Else had not tried to catch you for my lover,
So contrary to all the laws you taught!

Long after I am dead, you may be lying
Endless hours awake some winter night,
While a sad outwearied moon is dying
In lonely rags and tatters of her light;
Sir, you may decide then I was right.

(February 14, 1953)

A Sword Named Joy

If you love me as I love you,
No knife can cut our love in two!

On Christmas Day I gave my lord
An old and wicked Persian sword
To cut his finger on; and he
Did cut it most obligingly,
But would not let me kiss it well.
On Christmas morning it befell,
And all the bells of Oxford then
Were crying goodwill unto men!
O it was very bad indeed
To bring a gift that made him bleed,
It was unchristian and inhuman;
But still, the creature's name is woman —
A knife is a true lover's gift,
Old poets say; and so with thrift
She saved her pennies, had no rest,
Till she had found of knives the best,
Curved as sweetly as her breast.
And he has hung it on his wall,
And yet, he loves her not at all.

If you loved me as I love you,
No sword could separate us two!

(February 23, 1953)

A Cat to a King

My lord, the key to a fairy hill,
Fernseed that makes invisible,
Twenty spells in a silver box,
A hand of glory to open locks,
A phoenix on its nest, a rune
That might call down the lady moon
To light upon your window-ledge
And make round eyes at you; the hedge
That fenced the Sleeping Beauty in
To keep your garden safe; a jinn
Shut in a bottle, a flying dragon,
The Water of Life in a diamond flagon,
Aladdin's lamp and Solomon's ring
And any other magic thing
I would have brought, I would indeed;
But you have all the magic you need.

My friend, I would have brought you wit;
Rattling parchments packed with it
As bees pack sweetness in their cells;
A thousand centuries' miracles
Of laughter, and of wisdom too,
And four words that are really true.
You might rede[7] the riddle that lies
In the Sphinx's sand-blind eyes,
Or number angels while they stood
On that old needle's point. I would
Make you the sole and shining heir
Of prophet and philosopher.
And yet why trouble Jew or Greek
For buried wisdom? When you speak
In jest or earnest, men take heed;
For you have all the wit you need.

7. "Rede" means to interpret.

My dear, I would have brought you this;
A wild wood-strawberry and a kiss,
Woman's trinkets, light and little;
Fingertips as cool as brittle
Ice, to soothe your eyelids shut
When your thoughts are heavy and hot,
And a few sonnets from my store
Of softly rhyming sighs. What more?
Why, coal being scarce, I might contrive
To have my body burnt alive
Some winter night to warm your hands.
Whatever else that love demands
Of life and death, I might have given —
My tears, my blood, my hope of Heaven.
And yet I must not weep or bleed;
You have all the love you need.

There is one grace in littleness,
To know its limits; I confess
I have often heard men sing
Of a cat looked at a king,
But never heard it mentioned that
The king was looking at the cat,
And yet how else should you espy
A thing so nearly nought as I?
I that have not all I need
Kneel now at your feet to plead
For what I am and cannot be
And for my gift, your charity;
For I have brought you from far lands
My broken heart and empty hands.

(Fall 1953?)

Whine from a Beggar

I, who have nothing for you, beg your leave
To come and look at you sometimes. I plead
Your pity and your charity; indeed
If I had courage, I might ask your love;

But being your tainted and unwanted slave,
Crave only such a privilege as cats
Claim of their kings; to look at you. For that's
The one necessity that I dare have;

Not what I want in terms of hell and heaven;
Not what my pride may tell me I am worth,
Nor what wild generosity might give
Unworthiness. Not paradise, or even
Such poor delight as women get on earth;
But only what I need, my love, to live.

(January 1, 1954)

Nightlong I Wrestled[8]

Nightlong I wrestled by the waterspring
In the yellow desert; all night long the angel
Under a splintering cruelty of stars
Strained against my loins. The sands
Gritted between our teeth; a jackal
Crouched by his rock, waited to crack our bones.

Nightlong the man in semblance of an angel
Writhed and cried against me; when dawn
Touched the harsh land to a moment's kindness

---

8. In this poem Davidman alludes to the biblical story of Jacob wrestling with the angel. See Genesis 32:22-32.

Of soft colors, and I held him
Between my hands ready to break, a trick
Left me crippled in the lion's danger.

Nevertheless I held him. The lion sun
Leered over the horizon, dried us like lizards
Flattened dead on the desert; I held him.
Sun ate me and licked my empty skull; I held him.
I hold him still. My name is Israel,
Prince who has power with God, and I prevail.

(February 26, 1954)

Such Being the Nature of the Beast

Such being the nature of the beast,
That even in the act of prayer,
When the great angel in the east
Descends the gold ethereal stair

To help her climb it, she will turn
From heavenly to earthly fire;
Behold, the priest has words that burn;
The more to him is her desire.

O even if the Christ you preach
Were to come off His cross to seek her,
She would not so much love the speech
As she must dote upon the speaker.

God made you with a mortal need;
You might someday be glad to see
How sweetly she will always heed
The prophet, not the prophecy.

(May 1954?)

Blessed Are the Bitter Things of God

Blessed are the bitter things of God
Not as I desire but as I need
He pricks my pride and lets my spirit bleed.

Blessed are the fevers of the heart.
He tries me with the heat and with the cold.
I will be tempered steel when I am old.

I made my weapons out of flowers and grass.
I snared my brother as he tried to pass.
Let the Lord's anger wither up the grass.

I made my words the servants of my lust.
Now let me watch unwinking, as I must,
How the Lord's hands crumble my words to dust.

Willful I wandered naked in the wind,
Crying to love for pity. Let me find
No loving kindness. I have not been kind.

Blessed are the dark hours of the Lord.
Only by justice can I pay my debt;
I am not ready for His mercy yet.

(1954-1955?)

Ballade of the King's Jester

Some men cry when they are hurt;
Some take comfort from a sword,
Find the life and watch it spurt;
Some revenge with the abhorred
Iron maiden, rack and cord;
Some with delicate disdain.

Murdered men have shrieked and roared;
I laugh most when most in pain.

Women stricken to the heart
Cringe and whimper — be on guard;
They will grovel in the dirt
Till they can stab. And girls have whored
And drunk their grief to death, and poured
Silly souls away in vain;
Devils' tears be their reward!
I laugh most when most in pain.

Saints and children, they will blurt
Forgiveness out, when they are gored
Through and through to make us sport;
Saints and children, looking toward
Heaven and the great adored
Face of God, do not complain.
Holiness I find too hard;
I laugh most when most in pain.

Envoy

Will you listen, good my lord?
The worm that wriggles in my brain
Whispers me a merry word;
I laugh most when most in pain.

(1954-1955?)

Sentimentalist

Nothing has gone as I would have it go,
and it is late, the sun is nearly down.
The wind is rising in the twilight pines,
and I am very tired. I do not love
tonight, the pale pink east or the first star,
or the young virgin moon or any man.
Not even myself. Nothing, tonight, but sleep.

And yet, let me be grateful for the shell
I found beside the path and carried back
though it broke in my pocket.
                              Let me give thanks to God
for the small things that bring healing at these times
when love and hate alike grow stale. Give thanks
for the one ant that clambers up the grassblade
and the one oakleaf that is turning red;
snailshells, spiderwebs, and acorn cups.

O God,
whose greatest gifts I have so much misused,
whose love I turned into lust, whose laughter
I have made poisonous with irony,
whose tears I have wasted on my self-made griefs,
blessed art thou for all these small perfections;
stay me with grassblades, comfort me with crickets,
blue jays, butterflies, and acorn cups.

(1954-1955?)

Let No Man

Let no man
who speaks your name
hang on that hook
a word of blame.

If my breast's cage
be broken open
by a bullet;
these things happen.

If my body
is put in the ground;
if my heart is
a naked wound

sour with blood,
festered with salt;
these things happen;
it's not your fault.

(1954-1955?)

LOVE SONNETS TO C. S. LEWIS[9]

Dear Jack:

Here are some sonnets you may care to read;
The trouble with them, as I think you'll see,
Is that I do the trick too easily,
In fifteen seconds from desire to deed;

For I can write the thing acceptably
So often, it is hard to write it well.
The greater magic fails. Facility
Is the worst curse the devils dream in hell.

Nevertheless I have made such and such
Rhymes in your honour, sir, and here's the lot;
And if you think the sum of it not much,
Remember it's the only gift I've got;
As our slang has it, funny as a crutch —
The verse may be a joke; the love is not.

(1954-1955?)

AMERICA, 1951

I
Begin again, must I begin again
Who have begun so many loves in fire
And ended them in dirty ash? Despair
Of treating you better than other men

Would take the taste of love out of my mouth
Before I had spoken half the lying word.
I would have loved you once if I had dared
And made a song of it. I'll save my breath

9. For background information on these sonnets, see the Introduction.

And save your peace; God love you! But for me,
I'll measure my affection by the drachm[10]
As men weigh poisons. Honoured sir, I am
Somewhat your friend; as far as courtesy

Requires, your servant; not at all your slave.
I love you far too well to give you love.[11]

(April 8, 1951)

II
Having loved my love tonight with you between,
My lord, I pray you of your courtesy
That I may give as much as he gives me;
Lie mouth to mouth, skin upon naked skin,

Joy upon joy. Love, it would not be love
If the disposing of it were not yours;
Give me away then wholly, let him have
A splendor uncorrupted by these tears.

Because you have my heart, he has my bed,
And let him have it then conditionless
With all my heart; nor ever let him guess
How I, staring above his quiet head,

Knew, in the lonely midnight afterward,
The terrible third between us like a sword.[12]

(1948 or 1949)

III
Love is this and that and always present
When you chew a solitary cud
Thinking what you would do if you could;

10. A very small quantity.
11. Another draft of this sonnet is titled "When It Was Already Too Late."
12. Another draft of this sonnet is titled "Premonition." A third draft includes at the end in Joy's hand this note: "In a moment of insight, for CSL."

Love is something poisonous and pleasant,
Love is a buzzing fly, love is a blink
Of the mind's eye; love is a cold drink
That burns your insides out, love is not much
But you will fall to ashes at its touch;

Love will empty you and love will fill you
With the fluids that keep your heart pumping
And your eyes alive and your nerves jumping;
Love will go crazy if the moon is bright.
You can be very sure it will not kill you,
But neither will it let you sleep at night.[13]

(March 1940)

IV
Let me not lie about it; there are worse pains.
There is seeing your children shot before your face.
There is being buried alive in the shallow graves
Where afterward the torn sods heaved in vain.
There is gripping the bars and staring out at the rain
With fear cutting your belly like a knife.
There are many deaths and several sorts of life
That are much worse than what I feel for you;
And yet this loss is loss, this love hurts too — [14]

A pinprick surely, fit to make a song of?
A nuisance like a cinder in the eye,
A fleabite; I would not do you the wrong of
Pretending that I sicken and must die.
Believe me, I am sound —
                              Why, no; I lie.

(September 1938?)

13. Another draft of this sonnet is titled "Definitions."
14. These nine lines also appear as stanza II in the poem "Notes on an Obsession."

ENGLAND, 1952

V
Since one must have something to be proud of,
Let it be that I have kept them warm
In my comfortable crook of arm;
I have not slapped them on the crying lips
When they came to me and bleated love
And weakness, and despair; I have been kind.
I have not left them in the naked wind;
I have been a harbour to their ships.

Everyone alive must stand in line
Sooner or later, slavering and starved,
Waiting at the door where love is doled
Piecemeal; angel, the next turn is mine.
Here I am, and what have I deserved?
Here I hunger, waiting; I am cold.

(1940?)

VI
My lord and love, the yellow leaves were sailing
Confusing sorrowful air and earth together
Between two rivers, in the wistful weather,
Sky changing, tree undressing, summer failing;

September. And the waterbirds were calling,
Heartbroken, harsh, under their reedy cover;
That was no golden season for lover and lover
But for dying light and bright things falling.

Even the bells in Magdalen tower[15] were ringing
Death to the drooping afternoon, and never
A merry note to comfort him, for neither

15. This refers to the famous tower at Magdalen College, Oxford, where Lewis was
a don from 1925 to 1954.

Angels nor larks had any heart for singing;

And yet, not too forlorn a memory:
Oxford, autumn leaves, and you, and me.[16]

(December 10, 1952)

VII

Cherwell in spate[17] and Isis[18] swirling brown
Among the willows and the water-voles
That cower for comfort in their flooded holes,
And skies of anger over Oxford town

Until the rain comes murderously down
Among the naked beeches. How the wind
Whips all our talk and laughter out of mind,
And time, far more than Thames, has power to drown

What was so much alive. I have forgot
Innumerable joys, that dreaming of
Might have made night less dreadful all the years
I am to bear without you. Even tears
Fade and leave blank eyelids; only not,
O love, this bitter endless pain, my love.[19]

(Christmas 1952)

VIII

I brought my love obedience; cupped my hand
And held submission to his thirsty mouth,
A cooling water in a burning land;
And he, being hot and desperate with drouth,[20]

---

16. Another draft of this sonnet is titled "First Meeting."

17. "Spate" indicates a flood or inundation.

18. The Cherwell River and the Isis River (or more accurately the Thames River) are the two principal rivers around which the city of Oxford has grown and flourished.

19. Another draft of this sonnet is titled "Sonnet of Memories."

20. Drought.

Deigned to bend his head and drink it up.
Love was the water, loneliness the thirst,
And my poor earthen soul could serve for cup
To offer comfort. He was glad at first,

Until the taste of water grew a bore
And a small coin of thanks too much to pay;
Whereat he led me to an open door
And sent me and my empty soul away,
Saying I must not love him any more;
But now at last I learn to disobey.[21]

(January 1953)

AMERICA, 1953

IX
If ever I go back to Headington
I'll go on foot, some breezy day in spring,
With new leaves winking at the yellow sun
And subtle sounds of water murmuring

A silver word. If ever I go back
I shall come lightly as a flower or leaf
Dancing on April wind — and bring you, Jack,
Something a little sweeter than my grief.[22]

There was a day I brought a load of pain
And dumped the lot upon your willing shoulder
And dried my tears; but if I come again
I shall be wiser, merrier, and older;

21. Another draft of this sonnet is titled "Sonnet of Misunderstandings" and ends with this note: "S. S. Franconia, Jan. 1953." *S. S. Franconia* is the name of the vessel Davidman sailed on when she returned to America after her frequent visits with Lewis in the fall of 1952.

22. This probably refers to Davidman having shared with Lewis the deteriorating state of her marriage to Bill Gresham.

O may the rooks caw to the rising sun
For joy, when I come back to Headington.[23]

(*February* 11, 1953)

X
Why, you may call the thing idolatry
And tell no lie; for I have seen you shine
Brighter than any son of man should be;
And trembled, and half-dreamed you were divine,

And knelt in adoration; willfully
I bring my pleasant gifts to the wrong shrine,
And little joy there is of it for me;
You are not God, and neither are you mine.

The pagan priesthood, honouring their Baal,
Slashed themselves till they bled, and so have I,
Yet neither they nor I to much avail;
The fire was out, and vacant was the sky.[24]

Sir, you may correct me with your rod.
I have loved you better than I loved my God.[25]

(*February* 14, 1953)

XI
You have such reasons for not loving me
As would persuade the sunfire to go out,
Divorce the moon from the obedient sea,
Make rain fall upward, lead the rose to flout

The amorous honeybees, and talk the wind
Out of a wandering life; as would compel

23. Another draft of this sonnet is titled "Hopeful Sonnet."
24. Here Davidman alludes to the confrontation between Elijah and the prophets of Baal recorded in 1 Kings 18. See especially 1 Kings 18:25-29.
25. Another draft of this sonnet is titled "On Her Love Saying That She Loved Him Too Well."

Satan to consort with angelkind
And Gabriel to wallow deep in hell.

The argument that keeps the sun in power
Over his children, makes the firefly glow,
Adorns the summer with her proper flower
And decorates the winter with his snow,

Makes dead men rise and promises come true —
Such reasons do I have for loving you.[26]

(February 14, 1953)

XII
I am not Queen Helen, sir; I have no gold
Framing the perfect sorrow of my face;[27]
The best of me is merely commonplace,
And I am tired, and I am growing old,

My mirror says. A woman gets destroyed
In little ways, by the slow little years;
What splendour I had once has been alloyed
With baser metal of my lusts and fears.

What I am saying is that I have nothing
To give you that you possibly could want;
A double handful of the barren earth

26. Another draft of this sonnet is titled "Of the Laws of Nature."

27. In Greek mythology Helen of Sparta — better known as Helen of Troy — was hailed as the most beautiful woman in the world. She married Menelaus, king of Laconia, a Greek province. Entranced by her beauty, the Trojan prince, Paris, kidnapped Helen and took her to Troy. Her legendary beauty, "the face that launched a thousand ships," resulted in the Trojan War in which Menelaus led Greek warriors against Paris and his allies. When Davidman says that she has "no gold, / Framing the perfect sorrow of my face," she introduces the notion that Lewis had a penchant for blondes (for instance, see below Sonnets XX, XXII, and XXXI). If this was the case (nowhere does Lewis write about his attraction to blondes), Davidman, as a brunette, felt at a disadvantage. Moreover, she may also have been having something of a private joke with Lewis since her own first name was Helen.

Is all I am, a skull touched up with paint,
A thing to move your laughter or your loathing;
Still, you may have my love for what it's worth.[28]

(August 1, 1953)

XIII

I said it did not hurt. My lord, I lied;
Painted my mouth into a smiling shape
Before the mirror, taught my heart to ape
Happiness; wore the dagger in my side

As if it were a jewel. Laughing-eyed
And light, I cheated you into belief;
I would not have you grieving for my grief,
And so I jested even while I died.

Such good intentions; now I roll in hell
My wheel of agony, and burning stones
Eat their slow acid way into my bones
Etching the secret that I would not tell;
Eternity may teach my idiot brain
Not to blaspheme against God's gift of pain.[29]

(March 20, 1953)

XIV

When I have said all the words, what shall I do?
When all the rhymes are paired and I have sung
Whatever tunes are nested in my tongue,
And have made all the promises, false and true —

When the sonnets are written and the night
Burns black to moonset and bright to sunrise,
And dawn strikes like murder at my aching eyes
With its intolerable bruise of light —

28. Another draft of this sonnet is titled "The Inveterate Present-Giver."
29. Another draft of this sonnet is titled "Non Dolet" (Latin for "no regrets").

Always, after the praying and the poor gabble
Of sobs, and the twisting in the lonely bed,
And the clever spiderwebs I weave in my head
To catch you with, I sit down at my table

And stare at nothing, neither God nor you;
Sir, at the end of words, what shall I do?[30]

(February 22, 1953)

XV

Is it not enough, insatiate heart,
That a most silver and miraculous horn
Stabbed you once with splendour, struck apart
Your ironbound defenses, and made glad
The outward thrust and rush of your freed blood?
That you were frozen neither quick nor dead
Between the worlds, till murdered and reborn
By that one rapture of the unicorn?

Must holiness be hunted like a beast,
Tricked like a man, entangled in a snare
Woven of such poor stuff as womanhair?
Must you try to trap him in your bed,
A fire and valour to appease the lust
Of your cold empty arms? and yet you must.[31]

(January 8, 1953)

XVI

At the last hour the few important things
She kept firm hold of, had not much to do
With what she said and suffered, what he knew
Or thought about it all; or even love.
When they marched her to the king of kings
It was not these that she was dreaming of.

---

30. Another draft of this sonnet is titled "To My Love Who Told Me to Write Verses."
31. Another draft of this sonnet is titled "Apropos of the Unicorn."

She had outlived the agony of wonder
What he was really like inside his head,
Forgotten the harsh nights and lonely bed
While the long meteors died without a trace
Down the abyss of sky, and all her pains
Forgotten, when the angel came to thresh
Her spirit from her bones. One thing remains,
One arrow still may burn, while flesh is flesh;
The accidental beauty of his face.[32]

(*September 1938?*)

ENGLAND, 1954

XVII
Love, the world is ending; love, the night
Creeps foaming up the beaches, and no moon
To comfort us with mockeries of light
Survives in heaven. Love, we shall lie down soon;

Cold, cold the funeral wind. And of our bones
What shall be made but rubbish? Never rain
Whimpers to this trash in undertones
Of resurrection; spring comes not again

And none remember her. Now the ripe world
Crisps to a cinder while we watch; the sea
Shrivels into an icy serpent, curled
About our courage, and the Wolf runs free.

Yet one eternal moment let us stand
Against the encroaching dark. Give me your hand.[33]

(1938?)

32. This is a slight variation on the sonnet form since it contains fifteen lines rather than the normal fourteen lines. This poem also appears as stanza III in the poem "Notes on an Obsession."

33. Another draft of this sonnet is titled "Fimbulwinter." In Norse mythology, Fim-

XVIII

I think, my lad, you learn your charity
By rote and not by heart. 'Tis very well
For flights of angels, as I hear you tell,
To shower love on all men equally;

But you and I were made for other ends,
And you are something short of angel yet;
And if you smile upon the thing you hate,
'Tis kinder to your enemies than friends.

Love universal is love spread too thin
To keep a mortal warm; and when you wear
One smile for all, you freeze me with despair;
For my poor woman's wits cannot begin

To know if I'm a pleasure or a bore;
Less charity, my angel, might be more.

(February 23, 1954)

XIX

Here are three pair of wings caught in one net;
Three sets of silken feathers, as the bird
Stoops to the fowler's lure, and most ill met;
My love and I, with Christ to make the third.

And one of us has mud-bedabbled wings,
And one of us has wings washed clean as sun;
And one of us planned this and other things
Before the howling planets were begun.

Here are three unlikely birds indeed!
A jackdaw[34] in a peacock company

---

bulwinter (or harsh winter) was a three-year winter (with no intervening summers)
ushering in Ragnorak, the final battle that would end the world.

34. The common name of the daw, a small crow that frequents old buildings and
church towers; it is easily tamed and taught to imitate the sound of words.

I strut, until they peck me and I bleed,
Since I am black and they are bright to see;

Yet I've a fire at heart shall make me shine
Fit for my human love — or my divine.

(1954-1955?)

XX

My love, who does not love me but is kind,
Lately apologized for lack of love,
Praising the fire and glitter of my mind,
The valour of my heart, and speaking of

Affection, admiration, bitter scraps
Men fling the begging woman at the door
When hunger lends her courage and she raps
Loud at their consciences. — Why, there was more;

He said that I had beauty of a sort
Might do for other men, but not for him.
At which the grinning devils had their sport
And tore me shrieking, limb from bleeding limb;

To be rejected, O this worst of wounds,
Not for love of God, but love of blondes![35]

(January 22, 1954)

XXI

This that was a woman in its time
Loved you before you pulled its long hair out
By the bloody roots, punctured its eyes to slime
With sharp contempt, and neatly cut its throat

And hung the carcass downward by its heels
To drain, and fed it to a bird you kept

35. Another draft of this sonnet is titled "IV Gentlemen Prefer..."

Tame and called a phoenix. Pleasant meals
The feathered creature had before it slept

And left the tattered ribs to fill with air,
The shattered brain to light the naked skull
With a last mockery of life. Despair
Might think your leavings fit for burial;
And yet the horror is a woman still;
It grieves because it cannot stroke your hair.

(1938?)

XXII

It is not his fault he does not love me;
It is not his fault he does not know
Any anesthetic word to give me
When the devil makes him tell me so;

It is not my fault either. If I had
Brighter-coloured eyes and paler hair,
I might, it seems, be turned to gold and glad
By the same luck that leads me to despair.

Whose fault, then? Let the man have his Heaven
He cries for; as for me, I shrug, and pray
Some angel may announce he is forgiven
His good intentions on the judgment day,
While I go down beneath the fatal rod;
For even then I shall not pardon God.[36]

(1954-1955?)

XXIII

Lord, when you laid your treasure on my back
To carry for myself, you did not say
What pricks and thorns set thick along the way
Would scratch the heart out of me; how the track

---

36. Another draft of this sonnet is titled "The Problem of Pain."

Went wandering uphill in a thirsty land
Forever, how in bitter night the moon
Would smile contempt, and in the brazen noon
The sun blaze laughter at the naked sand

To see a laden fool crawling through pain;
How the unburdened men with envious eyes
Would mock at me dying beneath my prize.
Lord, you must take your treasure back again;

A precious gift, and I shall mourn its loss;
But only You have strength to bear the Cross.[37]

(January 22, 1954)

XXIV
When I first loved you, daylight sang and blazed
With angels; the incarnate miracle
Rang in my heart like ocean in a shell,
The sky was loud with God. And I, amazed

At choiring heaven, learned what I must do
With my one talent that had gone to waste,
Unwanted gold. I spent my love at last,
Brought it to God in bringing it to you.

This was the only music I could make Him;
My pitiable, small, and commonplace
Whimper of your name. You heard, and trod
That crying down, and taught me to forsake Him.
Love, you have sent me back to my own place,
A silence where there is not even God.[38]

(February 16, 1954)

37. Another draft of this sonnet is titled "Backslider."
38. Another draft of this sonnet is titled "The Sweet Cheat Gone."

XXV

Woman, stop complaining. He is gone;
You will not have him back for all your weeping.
The man is not for you, and whether dawn
Find you awake in tears, or find you sleeping

With tears dried on your eyelids, makes no matter,
Since tears will buy you nothing but his prayers.
Though you were resolute enough to shatter
The bars of hell, though you could climb the stairs

Of heaven to the top, you should not have him.
He is God's lover not yours, and he is fled
Beyond the ultimate stars. In God's name, leave him
To Christ, to angels, to the risen dead ...

No, follow. Some day he may need to use
The tatters of your soul to wipe his shoes.[39]

(*February* 2, 1954)

XXVI

I have wrenched sonnets out of my great pain
Nightly; as men dig gold. The angry rock
Breaks their fingerbones; the bitter rain
Leaches away their gains; the cruel clock

Counts their minutes on its hands, and they
Dribble to death, while grains of treasure lie
Useless to them, but shrewdly stored away
For unknown followers to find. So I

39. Another draft of this sonnet is titled "Ich Grolle Nicht" (German for "I bear no grudge" or "I do not chide"). Drawn from the well-known sixteen-song cycle of Robert Schumann, *A Poet's Love* (1840), Davidman's title "Ich Grolle Nicht" is from the seventh song in the cycle; the texts for the sixteen songs are from the *Lyrisches Intermezzo* (1822-1823) of Heinrich Heine.

Store my memories of you. The gold,
The sweet, the dreadful; how I took your arm
And climbed a hill of bracken all aflame
With sunset lights. Some woman who is cold
In bed may use my words to keep her warm
Some future night, and recall my name.[40]

(January 31, 1954)

XXVII

Dear cruelty, you should have wanted more;
You should have cut me into scraps of gold
To pay your taxes with, or burnt me for
A bonfire to defend you from the cold;

Drunk me for wine or eaten me for bread,
Made spillikins[41] of my small fingers; thence
You should have brought me naked to your bed
And got your sons on my obedience.

Instead you put my hunger on a ration
Of charitable words, and bade me live
On air, and wear a mask of smiles to dress
The bare indecency of desolation;
You asked for nothing, you would only give.
Dear cruelty, you should have wanted less.

(February 18, 1954)

XXVIII

O I did wrong to wake you from that sleep
Whose splendour glimmered on your eyelids; wrong
To thrust between you and the airy shapes
That fill your dreams with rainbows. You belong

Where lions are not real enough to hurt;
Not in a tangled web of sins and groans,

40. Another draft of this sonnet is titled "Powerful Rhyme."
41. Splinters.

This waking world, where I must see my heart
Smashed in daylight on the cobblestones.

I thought you turned in sleep and cried my name
To be a playmate for you in a land
Too lovely and too lonely for most men;
I woke you to my disillusion. Blame
The credulous heart that must misunderstand;
For I did wrong. Sleep, sleep, and dream again.

(February 18, 1954)

XXIX

There was a man who found a naked tree
Sleeping in winter woods, and brought her home,
And tended her a month in charity
Until she woke, and filled his quiet room

With petals like a storm of silver light,
Bursting, blazing, blended all of pearl
And moonshine; he, in wonder and delight,
Patted her magic boughs and said: Good girl.

Thereafter, still obedient to the summer,
The tree worked at her trade, until behold
A summer miracle of red and gold,
Apples of the Hesperides upon her,
Sweeter than Eden and its vanished bowers ...
He said: No, no, I only wanted flowers.

(1954-1955?)

XXX

Talking to you as one crucified thief
To another; Lord, will you not tell me why
You have spread-eagled me on a black sky,
Nailed through my fingerbones with nails of grief

Forever? What are you buying with my pain?
Is it worth jewels, can you ransom souls

With this poor coin of wounds, these bleeding holes
Knocked in a human heart? If you can gain

A silver population for your heaven,
You are welcome to all you rob me of;
You may filch the lot and be forgiven,
Blood and breath and laughter, tears and love.
Only this one prayer; do not let me die
An idiot sacrifice, not knowing why!

(March 1, 1954)

XXXI
The God I worshipped said: Woman, no tricks.
Such magic as you have of lip and eye
And fingers straying on a sleeve, and sly
Caressing words, forbear. You must not vex

My prophet at his prayers. Though you should die
Strung on the shrieking wires of your own nerves
Like a flayed animal, endure, and serve.
And I found strength to answer: I will try.

Then he, God's prophet, like a drunken sailor
Choosing in a brothel from a crowd
Of whores: What, little Brownie, there? Not half!
I'll have a blonde or nothing! Quick, unveil her!
And far away within an evil cloud
I heard the thing that I had worshipped laugh.

(May 9, 1954)

XXXII
Has He made you a fisher of women, then?
Was it He who taught you how to bait
The hook you caught me through the heart with? When
You armed yourself with glittering lure and net

And murderous gaff, and angled for a girl
With what was almost a magician's rod

In dim poetic seas of dreaming pearl,
All this was to the greater glory of God?

My friend, if it was sin in you and me
That we went fishing for each other in
The troubled waters of life, let honesty
Compel ourselves to carry such a sin;

And let us not, with self-deceiving lies,
Kiss and betray Him to His enemies.   (1954-1955?)

XXXIII
Forgive me that I turn my bitter tongue
Against you sometimes. None of them are true,
The harsh and jagged words. If there was wrong,
It was done by God and not by you;

He used you for His knife. Since I am dying
Of His long vivisection, need you wonder
If I cannot forbear a moment's crying
Against the steel that saws my throat asunder?

Why blame yourself? You did not make the world.
Blame Him who let it be so badly made
That I, because I love you, must be hurled
To bloody ruin by your helping arm;
I know you never meant me any harm;
And yet, I know that I have been betrayed.

                                                        (1954-1955?)

XXXIV
No, it was neither you nor God, but I
Whose nature drove the dagger in my side
So deadly near my heart; if I should die
Of loving you, call it a suicide.

Had I the choice of being otherwise
Than this meek amorous wretch? I cannot know;

I can be certain that I would not choose
Any lesser gate of death than you.

If I rebel, it is not that I crave for
More of this world's sweet poison in my food;
Only, when I see my children sleeping,
I think I have a task to keep alive for;
But they and I must take our chance on God.
Let it be as He wills, and no more weeping.

(March 10, 1954)

XXXV

Poor child, who read a book of magic once,
And tried such games as walking on the waves,
Distilling essences of stars and suns,
And conjuring dead women from their graves

To skip a sarabande[42] about you! When,
As children will, you wearied of your play
And would have sent them to their holes again,
How sad to find they would not go away!

No good to cross yourself, no help to run,
No use to mumble prayers beside your bed;
You're haunted by a woman-skeleton
With pits of grief for eyes, nodding its head
And clicking comments bitter as a bone;
Child, it is dangerous to raise the dead.

(May 9, 1954)

XXXVI

The monstrous glaciers of your innocence
Are more than I can climb; I might have braved
Platoons of dragons, or a fiery fence,
But walls of ice defeat me. Being saved

42. A slow, stately dance.

More by childishness than chastity,
You might remember, merely to enliven
Your prayerful nights, that hell, for some, may be
A colder, not a warmer place than heaven.

O my Antarctica, my new-found land[43]
Of woman-killing frost! but could I dare
More than the least touch of a casual hand;
Could I but come upon you in your bed
And kiss you at my leisure — why, my lad,
You might forget the colour of my hair.

(May 9, 1954)

XXXVII
I wish you were the woman, I the man;
I'd get you over your sweet shudderings
In two such heartbeats as the cuckoo sings
His grace-notes in! I play the games I can

With eye and smile; but not in womanhood
Lies power to lay hands on you and break
Your frosty inhibitions; it would take
Centaurs' force, transfusions of sun's blood.

Call it your virtue if you like; but love
Once consummated, we recover from;
Not so, love starved forever. Thus you have,
With this device of coldness, made me tame;
Your whipped adoring bitch, your tethered slave
Led on the twin leashes of desire and shame.

(May 9, 1954)

43. Here Davidman reveals her close knowledge of the poetry of John Donne, especially his elegy "Going to Bed," where a man urges his female companion to join him in bed as he delightedly watches her undress. In her reference to Lewis's "cold" responses to her desires for emotional and physical intimacy, she sends him an inside joke since she alludes to these lines in Donne's elegy: "License my roving hands, and let them go, / Behind, before, above, between, below. / O my America, my new-found-land, / My king-dome, safeliest when with one man man'd, / My Myne of precious stones" (ll. 25-29).

XXXVIII

Yes, I know: the angels disapprove
The way I look at you. Creation weeps,
Observing how my naughty finger creeps
Along your sleeve. On this unlucky love

Of mine, even merry Satan will not smile,
Nor waste a gilded flame on such a thing
As you have left blackened and shriveling;
The husk of me is hardly worth his while.

But one day, riding on the upper deck
Of a large, red, respectable Oxford bus
You in the seat in front, and I behind
Coveting the back of your nice neck
Where your hair curls — why, I might lean and kiss;
Somehow I do not think that God would mind.

(1954-1955?)

XXXIX

Do not be angry that I am a woman
And so have lips that want your kiss, and breasts
That want your fingers on them; being human
I need a heart on which my heart can rest;

Do not be angry that I cry your name
At the harsh night, or wear the darkness through
With blind arms groping for you in a dream;
I was made flesh for this, and so were you.

Quarrel with God if you like, but not with me,
That hands beaten impotently for three years
Against an iron door, could still caress
The naked body of love with ecstasy,
And might have ways to teach you tenderness
More than you have learned from all your prayers.

(1954-1955?)

XL

I brought lilies in my hands, tigerspotted,
Bloodthroated lilies, coloured with gold and death,
Stained with the opal world, veined and netted
With patterned pride. I waited, holding my breath.

He would not have them. Then I dipped my lilies
In vats of purity, freezing them to crystal
Lightbearers, chalices of morning chill,
Mystery silver as dew on every petal;

He would not have them. Down, you lilies, down,
Let hellmouth eat your beauty. Woman, take
Two nails instead and hammer for his sake
The spikes where they should go, till there has grown
Within each empty hand a brilliant rose
Of sacrificial blood. He might have those.[44]   (*March 30, 1954*)

XLI

Love me or love me not; nevertheless autumn
Scatters bright bonfires of leaves upon the ground,
Patterns with swirls of leaves the river water;
We shall find horse-chestnuts, bright and brown,

The right shape for your fingers and mine. You cannot
Love me at all, but there will be spring days
Striped with cloud and daffodil like banners;
We'll drink our beer among anemones

Another time, perhaps. And I shall call
The laughter that lies sleeping in your voice
To wake, or finish poems when you begin them;
The sterile years have starry moments in them.
Love me or love me not, the leaves will fall,
And we shall walk them down. I have my joys.   (*May 1954*)

44. Another draft of this sonnet is titled "Flower Piece."

XLII
You are all the gold of all the rocks
Precious in my fingers; brighter things,
Lucid gold, netted in a brook,
Of the rising sun; gold when the oriole sings

Burning in his throat and on his wings;
A flame, a dance of stars, a merry splendour
Of sun on mountaintops, a laugh that rings
Out of God's great mouth; a summer thunder

Of revelation. How I tantalize
Hunger with praising you, who gleam so far
Beyond my greedy reach; yet, now and then,
By God's grace, I am given a moment when
The shadow of pain is lifted from my eyes
And I rejoice to see how gold you are.

(May 1954)

XLIII
What a fool I was to play the mouse
And squeak for mercy! What had you to give
So small a creature when it wanted love?
Kind follows kind, lion to lioness

Calls in his season, not to little things
That cower with their bellies to the ground.
Lately you thundered magic that unbound
My nature; now I snarl at bearded kings

Upon Assyrian friezes, prop the doors
Of Agamemnon's town, provide a skin
That Hercules can wrap his valour in;
Lioness to drowsy lion roars!
Wake up and take the sun! His golden paws
Itch like mine to play with you. 'Ware claws!

(1954-1955?)

XLIV

Now, having said the words that can be said,
Having set down for any man to see
My blood and body in plain poetry;
Having displayed my sickness; brought to bed

Publicly; what advantage shall I have
To be thus naked to the questioner?
How shall it serve, how shall it profit her
Gaining the kingdom, locked outside your love?

Open your door, lest the belated heart
Die in the bitter night; open your door,
My lord. Admit the traveller to the fire.
Here is the quiet light, the silent shore
Beyond the foaming world; here is the chart
Of the last journey, past the last desire.[45]

(*November* 1939)

---

45. Another draft of this sonnet is titled "Postscript."

Appendix: Poetic Verse Patterns

As a young woman, Joy Davidman translated dozens of French poems by Francis Jammes, Charles L'Orleans, Henri de Regnier (see "Odelette" on pp. 6-7), Paul Verlaine (see "Clair de Lune" on pp. 5-6 and "Il Pleure dans Mon Coeur" on pp. 122-23), and François Villon. Verlaine, in particular, was a favorite. Given her deep affection for these French poets, it is not surprising that in many of her poems she employed French verse forms.

Ballade: Perhaps the most popular of all French verse forms, the ballade normally contains three stanzas and a final envoy. A refrain occurs at the end of each stanza and the envoy, and only three (in some cases four) rhymes are permitted — always occurring in the same position in each stanza. Often the envoy offers a climactic conclusion. Although stanzas can be of varying length, the most frequent is a verse of eight lines rhyming *ababbcbc* with *bcbc* for the envoy.

Rondeau: The rondeau is a French verse form containing fifteen lines, with the ninth and fifteenth lines being a short refrain. Only two rhymes are permitted throughout the three stanzas: *aabba aabc aabbac*.

Sestina: Another French verse form, the sestina is one of the most complex. The typical sestina consists of six six-line stanzas and a three-line envoy. Rather than relying upon rhyme within each stanza, the sestina relies upon a fixed pattern of end-words. The end-words in each stanza must be the same, but they are arranged in a different, prescribed sequence each time. Thus if the end-words in the first stanza are 1-2-3-4-5-6, the second would be 6-1-5-2-4-3, the third would be 3-6-4-1-2-5, the fourth would be 5-3-2-6-1-4, the fifth would be 4-5-1-3-6-2, the sixth would be 2-4-6-5-3-1, and the envoy would be 5-3-1 (repeating the last three end-words of the sixth stanza) and also would embed 2-4-6 within the lines of the envoy.

Sonnet: Originally an Italian verse form, the fourteen-line sonnet was popularized in English during the sixteenth century by Edmund Spenser and William Shakespeare. Two forms of the sonnet resulted. While both forms usually employ iambic pentameter, the Italian sonnet's typical rhyme scheme is *abba abba cde cde*; although the sestet may sometimes be *cdd cdd* or *cdcdcd*, only five rhymes are permitted throughout the poem. Rhetorically, the first eight lines (octave) introduce a problem or dilemma while the last six lines (sestet) move toward a resolution or acceptance. The English sonnet's rhyme scheme is *abab cdcd efef gg*; seven rhymes are permitted throughout the poem. While the English sonnet sometimes follows the same rhetorical pattern as the Italian, often the three quatrains contain metaphors or similes related to the problem while the final couplet offers a witty, terse, or startling resolution.

Villanelle: In still another French verse form, the villanelle contains nineteen lines, uses only two rhymes, and repeats two lines according to a prescribed pattern. Line 1 is repeated as lines 6, 12, and 18; line 3 as lines 9, 15, and 19. The first and third lines appear as a rhymed couplet at the end of the poem. The scheme of rhymes and repetitions is *abA aba aba abaA*.

Index of Titles

Index of First Lines